A HIGHLY ARBITRARY,

THOROUGHLY

OPINIONATED GUIDE TO

LISTENING TO—AND

ENJOYING!—SYMPHONY,

OPERA, AND CHAMBER

MUSIC

MICHAEL
WALSH

WHO'S AFRAID OF CLASSICAL MUSIC?

CASTLE
BOOKS

This edition published in 2004 by
CASTLE BOOKS ®
A division of Book Sales, Inc.
114 Northfield Avenue
Edison, NJ 08837

Published by arrangement with and permission of
Simon & Schuster Inc.
1230 Avenue of the Americas
New York, New York 10020

Originally published by FIRESIDE.
FIRESIDE and colophon are registered trademarks of
Simon & Schuster, Inc.

Library of Congress Cataloging-in-Publication Data

Walsh, Michael (Michael Allen)
    Who's afraid of classical music? / Michael Walsh.
        p. cm.
    "A Fireside book."
    1. Music—History and criticism. 2. Music
appreciation.
    I. Title.
    ML 160.W256 1968
    781. 1'7—dc20   89-35440
                                                           CIP
                                                          MN

ISBN 0-7858-1737-9

Printed in the United States of America

Designed by Janis Ray Lotwin
"Bach and Handel at the Wall" was originally published in
Time on March 25, 1985.   Copyright © 1985, Time Inc.
Reprinted with permission.

CONTENTS

PREFACE

This book grows out of a common question and a felt need: how should you listen to classical music? And why? During my 16 years as a practicing music critic, I must have been asked this hundreds of times. Otherwise perfectly intelligent and acculturated people, many of them very successful in their own fields of endeavor, seem to feel that there is some secret to listening to classical music, some trick or innate talent. Even if they like music, and attend concerts or the opera, they believe that their opinions of what they have heard are not as good or as worthy—in short, as informed—as mine. (Others, of course, feel their opinions are a good deal better than mine, and don't hesitate to let me know it.) It's as if classical music were a Masonic lodge, with a secret handshake and password shared only by initiates. Which gets us back to our original questions. How? Why?

I'm not going to answer here. I hope I have addressed these issues satisfactorily in this book, which is frankly written for and directed at the layman. You will find little scholarly discourse contained herein, and infrequent technical discussions; you will, on the other hand, find iconoclastic asides and frequent cultural references to everything from Arnold Schwarzenegger movies to the wit and wisdom of Yogi Berra. (Two tickets to the concert of your choice to the first reader who can spot them all. Transportation not included.)

Many of my sentiments are unorthodox, and some are sure to irritate. My tone is light, my attitude occasionally irreverent. But my intention, I hope, is serious and sincere: to bring the novice to an understanding and love for the world of classical music, and to help him and her make it a part of their lives.

To accomplish this objective, I have adopted an unconventional structure. *Who's Afraid of Classical Music?* is meant to be conversational, as if you and I were sitting together, talking music. Although I have included biographical sketches of the most important or interesting composers, as well as a prolonged discussion of the works in my basic repertoire chapter, I have tried to avoid the laundry-list approach to music education, or the Chinese menu theory, or any of the other tried-and-untrue stratagems that have traditionally been used by the well-meaning music appreciators who were the bane of our high school existences. Nor is my tack encyclopedic. There are plenty of those books around, including those of David Ewen and radio commentator Karl Haas's *Inside Music.* But they both presuppose some knowledge of the classical music world. This book assumes none. It is completely a reflection of my own likes, tastes, interests and prejudices and makes no pretense to either completeness or fairness.

I have many people to thank, especially my family, who bravely forsook weekends, holidays and even Christmas to help me while I was writing; my wife Kate's suggestions and proofreading were invaluable. My friend Mark Glabman triggered the subject of Chapter Three when he asked me in a Paris bar one day, "How *do* you listen to classical music?" (Paris does that to people.) Thanks also to my agent, the peerless Don Congdon, and to my editor at Fireside, Barbara Gess, whose patience was much appreciated as I revised, fiddled, reconstructed, and added *just one more work* to the repertoire chapter. Even then, I know I left some out.

I also owe a debt to my employer, *Time* magazine, whose resources have allowed me to travel the world several times over these past eight years in pursuit of music stories. With a coincidence that bordered on the astounding, and never failed to amaze my co-workers, the stories very often were to be found in glamorous European capitals and exotic Asian locations.

And last, I would like to thank my principal editor at *Time*, Martha Duffy, who has always held my work up to her rigorous high standards and, at great pains to both of us, has made me a better writer and critic. "Don't write for your colleagues, write for the reader," she tells me nearly every week; any failings in this regard are entirely the fault of the author. In revenge, I have dedicated this book to her.

Finally, a word of thanks to my colleague, Henry Pleasants, whose incendiary works are quoted in this book, and whose philosophy permeates it. When I mentioned to Henry in London some time ago that I was writing this book as a kind of sequel to *The Agony of Modern Music*, he smiled and said, "Don't expect to get any thanks for it. I didn't."

And now, on with the show.

New York City–Munich
February 1989

INTRODUCTION

Let's face it: you hate classical music. No, not exactly hate; that is too strong. You used to hate classical music: too square, too long, too boring. Today you are, shall we say, indifferent to it. All right, not exactly indifferent: you do like the *Elvira Madigan* piano concerto by Mozart, as well as that little thing of Bach's that George Winston plays, and the lick from Strauss's Alsosprachwhatayacallit that Kubrick used at the beginning of *2001*. Come to think of it, maybe it is growing on you, a little.

Yes, it is. Admit it. When entertaining, you feel a little déclassé slipping on the latest New Age musings as background music when you know there is something better, something with more, well, class. You really could be getting greater use out of that new compact disc player you just bought. And, yes, on Sunday morning you do like to relax with the paper over brunch and Vivaldi on the local classical station. So indifferent is not exactly the right word.

Let's try ignorant. Let's try intimidated. Let's try afraid. Yes, that's it! Ignorant, intimidated and afraid! Ignorant of the difference between mezzoforte and a mezzo-soprano; intimidated by the cognoscenti talking about various Vladimir Horowitz performances like wine critics arguing the merits of chateaus and vintages; and afraid of making a fool of yourself by pretending to expertise in the one art form that cannot be convincingly faked. (Think about it: have you ever met anyone who claimed to know something about classical music when he or she knew there was a real expert in the room? Bet not. It's like trying to fake baseball statistics with a Rotisserie League champion.)

Longing as you are to cast off the adolescent trappings of your life and be seen, as you head into mid-life, as a man or woman of *gravitas*, you nevertheless have tended to steer clear of classical music. Now, caught up in the guilt-inducing wave of What Every American Should Know, you are busy dusting off your Tolstoy, brushing up your Shakespeare, and looking at the paintings in the local museum with a keener eye. But music remains the great mystery: everybody knows what a BMW is, but BWV. . . . The time has come, however, to exorcise this primal anxiety, to put aside the playthings of childhood and stride purposefully into the prime of your life.

I'm not here to tell you that classical music is good for you, the way your high school music appreciation teacher probably did. The memorable ad for radio station KFAC in Los Angeles, which showed a Mr. Hyde slob transformed into a Dr. Jekyll boulevardier just by tuning in, notwithstanding, classical music will not necessarily make you better looking, or smarter, or more success- ful. No one today ought to think that classical music is high in moral fiber and good for the soul. Music is morally neutral; Stravinsky even once famously asserted that it has no content at all other than that of abstract sound. Music does not create a breed of ethical supermen. Indeed, it hardly needs pointing out that some perfectly dreadful people have been prominent in classical music (the composer Richard Wagner, for one, a man who thought the world owed him a living. Actually, it sort of did). Instead, classical music should be seen as one of life's most exhilarating and satisfying sensory pleasures, and your discovery of it through records, concerts and reading will turn out to be a voyage of self-discovery. If music makes you a better person along the way, great, but there are no guarantees. What it will make you is a more sophisticated, mature and happier person—and if that makes you better looking, smarter and more successful, so be it. Remember, John Barrymore went from Jekyll to Hyde without special effects. So, in reverse, can you: it's all a matter of attitude.

In a way, you are lucky that you are just now getting involved with serious music. Lucky because, not long ago, your negative impressions of it might have been almost exactly right. Until fairly recently, the classical music scene was pretty much a closed circle of worshipful acolytes celebrating the holy mysteries of an arcane art form. (For more about this, see Chapter Six.) But the most exciting—and salutary—development in the past thirty years has been the vast expansion of the definition of what constitutes serious music. One practical benefit is that the dreadful snootiness and narrow-mindedness that have so damaged classical music's image in this century is finally on the wane: every time you see the little old ladies of both sexes streaming out of a concert hall because they are offended by a new piece, chalk up the sight as a victory for right thinking people the world over.

It doesn't matter whether the piece is something old like Anton Webern's *Symphony;* something new, like the latest work by Terry Riley; something borrowed, as when the punk-rock classical ensemble from San Francisco, the Kronos String Quartet, ends its concerts with Jimi Hendrix's *Purple Haze;* or even something blue, like Duke Ellington's *Black, Brown, and Beige.* The point is: classical music is *not* simply what one hears in the symphony halls and opera houses in America. That would be as limiting as to say that food is what you find only in the great French restaurants. What the U.S. orchestras and opera companies play is merely a subset of the great, vast world of classical music that lies beyond the comfy, safe, known universe that they generally inhabit. But art music is also to be heard in the polyphonic pyrotechnics of medieval and renaissance music, in the artless elegance of a Scott Joplin rag and in the minimalist meditations of Steve Reich and Phil Glass. In the folk music of Hungary, in New Orleans jazz, in the smooth vocalism of Frank Sinatra, and in the disquieted songs of Dire Straits. So you think you know nothing about serious music? You already know a lot more than you suspect.

Despite all this, you remain unconvinced. "I'm interested in classical music, but . . ." Which is precisely the point. This book is not another sanctimonious lecture on the ineffable genius of Mozart, nor a laundry list of composers, nor another bluffer's guide to steer you, the tyro, past the perilous shoals of high-toned party chitchat. Rather, I hope that it will lead you to music gently and enjoyably with a practical mix of information, opinion, recommendations and commentary. I want you to love music as much as I do. But don't expect a reverent walk through a museum. We're here to bust a few icons. Of course it is important to introduce the great composers and discuss their major works. But as Chili Davis once said of Dwight Gooden, "He ain't God, man." Mozart wrote obscene letters to his cousin and scatalogical canons for chorus, Beethoven emptied his chamber pot into his piano, Liszt was a satyr, Chopin lived with a female transvestite, Brahms could have sex only with prostitutes, venereal disease drove both Schumann and Smetana insane and killed Schubert. This is not a cloistered order of monks we're talking about here.

About the O-word: opera. Long before the Marx Brothers did their number on *Il Trovatore* in *A Night at the Opera,* folks have enjoyed themselves by making fun of this most sublime and most risible musical form: if you think you hate classical music, you are *positive* that you hate opera. But actually, opera is the most rewarding, as well as the most challenging and complex, art form, and a little investment of time and patience will pay huge dividends. We'll get you into opera in a hurry, and before you can say *Un Ballo in Maschera* you'll be ready for the *Ring* cycle—or at least for *La Boheme.*

Naturally, we'll discuss the basic repertoire—those forty or so elementary pieces that everyone should know: selected symphonies by Haydn, Mozart, Beethoven, and Brahms; operas by Mozart, Verdi and Puccini; chamber music by Beethoven and Schubert. But what lies beyond this conservative, safe selection of tunes? This book will tell you.

And how will we come by our new sophistication? Through recordings, primarily. We live in an age in which the dominant musical medium is the record player/phonograph. You have probably heard a thousand records for every live concert you've attended. Let's not bewail this, but face up to the opportunities and perils that recordings offer us.

The snobs will tell you that there is no substitute for live performance, which is true as far as it goes. But just as reading a Shakespeare play immeasurably enhances your enjoyment and understanding, so do recordings assist us in learning the great repertoire. You already own a CD player, and perhaps you have tested the hi-fi waters with a classical disc or two, since the digital medium was invented to capture the extreme dynamic range of classical music. Techies already have realized this, and no doubt classical compact discs are finding their way through doors that have never been darkened by Dvorak before—maybe even yours. I can't be there with you in the concert hall, but believe me, once you've developed your interest and knowledge even a little bit, a visit to the symphony or opera house is not far away.

(Speaking of snobs, please refer to the Appendix, which will give you some unorthodox ammunition to use when push comes to shove.)

Don't look to me for record-buying guidance, though. Nothing dates a book faster than record recommendations, especially these days, when record companies are being bought and sold like . . . like, well, the rest of the companies on Wall Street. The advent of the compact disc has meant that a tremendous amount of the old recorded repertoire is being lost as LPs gradually disappear from store shelves; I can't predict which classics will be deemed worthy of salvage on CD and which will not. But then, developing your taste in performance is one of the most important and valuable things you can do for yourself. It's fun, too.

Just as the tie-dyed rebels of the sixties have forsaken their bell-bottoms for the more sophisticated pleasures of fine wine, boutique beer and the Sharper Image catalog, so now are you cautiously sidling up to the sleek carriage of classical music, kicking its tires and yearning to take it for a test drive. *Who's Afraid of Classical Music?* will hand you the keys and put you in the driver's seat.

Ladies and gentlemen, start your engines!

1

OF CABBAGES, KINGS, AND KÖCHELS

Relax. You and I both know that you're ready to learn a little more about classical music. But you're not exactly sure *why*. So: Why?

Because classical music is one of the glories of Western civilization, that's why. Because no educated person should go through life without the acquaintance of Bach, Beethoven, and Brahms. Because a knowledge and love of classical music is the mark of a sophisticated man and woman. Because . . . well, because it will help you meet members of the opposite sex.

No, seriously. Have you ever been to a concert in Japan? The audience consists almost entirely of young men and women—mostly women. In Germany, young people flock to the Philharmonie in Berlin, to the Gasteig Center in Munich, to the avant-garde goings-on in Cologne. What do you think they're there for? Not just Beethoven or Berio.

Okay, this isn't Europe or Japan. This is America, land of TV, home of the couch potato. Here, the audience at classical concerts is mostly little old ladies, isn't it? So why should a red-blooded all-American like you care about some ancient history from Squaresville? Isn't classical music boring and irrelevant? And if anybody still wanted to listen to it, it would be on the Top Forty, right? And if it were *really* popular, orchestras wouldn't be going out of business, opera companies wouldn't always have their hands out fundraising, chamber concerts would draw as many people as Michael Jackson, and you might actually meet someone who listens to National Public Radio.

So you reiterate: *why?*

Because your premises, while superficially correct, are not germane, that's why. Now, I'm not here to tell you that classical music is as popular as Michael Jackson, or even Jermaine Jackson. But you might be surprised to know how popular it is. Orchestra subscriptions in just about any city you can name outnumber season ticket holders at the local ballpark. The annual budget of a major cultural institution like New York City's Metropolitan Opera or the Boston Symphony Orchestra is measured in tens of millions of dollars. Top performers earn big bucks: $40,000 per concert by violinist Itzhak Perlman, ninety percent of the gross receipts by pianist Vladimir Horowitz. There's major money involved in classical music and, considering the abysmally low level of government subsidy of the arts in the United States, somebody must be paying it.

Yes, really. There are as many symphony orchestras in this country as there are daily newspapers—more than 1,500 of them, staffed by dedicated players and administrators and attracting a loyal public that is as proud of the local orchestras as it is of the local football team. And not just in Podunk, either. Have you ever listened to a Clevelander talk about the Cleveland Orchestra? You'd think he was boasting about the Browns or the Indians. Come to think of it, though, the Cleveland Orchestra usually has a better year than either the Browns or the Indians. In fact, they are always in the top five.

Wait, there's more. In Boston, the local symphony is more than a hundred years old, and has long been a staple of the Hub's cultural life; an evening at Symphony is as traditional as a trip to the Fens to see the Sox. The San Francisco Opera, in one incarnation or another, dates back a century, to the time when giants roamed the earth: Enrico Caruso was in town in April 1906 to sing a performance when, early that morning, he was thrown violently out of his bed by the Great San Francisco Earthquake. As soon as he could, he fled town and never came back, but the opera lived on. And just think of the place Carnegie Hall holds in the popular imagination. (How do you get to Carnegie Hall?:

practice, practice, practice!) Classical music is not as obscure as you think.

I'll prove it. Remember Eric Carmen's *Never Gonna Fall in Love Again?* The tune is from Serge Rachmaninoff's *Second Symphony.* Half the tunes in the Broadway show *Kismet* are from the works of Alexander Borodin, such as his opera *Prince Igor.* Andrew Lloyd Webber uses a lick from Puccini's *Turandot* in his hit, *The Phantom of the Opera.* These tunes, and hundreds more like them, are not tough to like. And you always thought classical music had to sound ugly, like the *Grosse Fuge* by Beethoven.

That's *"Grow-suh Foo-guh."* Let's admit it: one of the most intimidating things about classical music is all those terrifying foreign words. Yes, I know you were terrible at languages in high school and, yes, German is tough. Still, you don't want to make a fool of yourself by saying "gross fudge" in polite company.

(Unfortunately for those of you who did fairly well in high school Spanish, there aren't many important Spanish composers. About the time that Philip II hung up his pantaloons, the Spaniards went into a cultural slump for about three hundred years. Aside from some lesser figures like Isaac Albeniz and Enrique Granados around the turn of this century, the pickings are fairly slim. As Yogi Berra, or somebody, once wondered: How come all great Spanish music was written by the French? Check it out. Ravel wrote the *Rapsodie Españole* and *Alborada del gracioso,* Chabrier wrote *España,* Debussy wrote *Soirée dans Grenada* and *Iberia*—and Bizet wrote *Carmen.* Convinced?)

Back to languages. Even without being fluent in French, Italian, and German, you can still figure this stuff out. You'll be surprised how fast you pick it up. I have a friend who speaks impeccable opera-libretto Italian and German. He knows how to say "Help!," "I'm dying," and "I love you" in three different languages—terrific if he ever meets a lady cop or doctor in Italy or Germany. The point I'm trying to make is that you can learn a lot very quickly, without having to enroll in Berlitz. Why, before you know it, you'll be saying *Die Vier Jahreszeiten* without batting an eye. That's *"Dee Fear Ya-re-tseye-ten."* I personally guarantee that you'll know how to pronounce the most important names and terms by the time I'm finished with you. Of course, Don Mattingly personally guaranteed the Yankees a pennant in 1988. But I'm not George Steinbrenner, thank God.

And you're just you. Former college radical—hi, Jerry!—now a professional with a good job—hi, Tom!—good spouse—hi, Jane!—nice home, nice car. You've even got 1.2 children and an Akita of distinction. So now I'm giving you something else to shoot for. Think of classical music the way you think of bodybuilding—you *do* pump iron, don't you? You start with the basic exercises, to build mass, then move on to the refinements to add definition. It's the same way in classical music. We'll start with the basic repertory—those works that have, as they say, stood the test of time—then fill out our profile with some choice connoisseur items. No pain, no gain: we're not going to fake anything—we're here to *learn*. But you're the one who has to put out the effort. It will take time and it will take patience; there's no immediate gratification here. Are you ready?

Then let's begin. What does "Op." mean?

You see this abbreviation all the time, with a number after it—Op. 4, Op. 125, etc.—after the title of a piece. You know, like Beethoven's *Hammerklavier Sonata*, Op. 106, or, even worse, his *Piano Sonata*, Op. 10, No. 3. One of them has a nickname, the other one has a number—it's enough to send you screaming back to *I Want to Hold Your Hand*.

But it's really quite simple. That forbidding abbreviation "Op." merely stands for *opus*, the Latin word for *work*. Its plural is *opera*, which has nothing to do with fat people singing. (I never said this would be logical.) Anyway, the Op. designation is usually not the composer's choice at all, but the publisher's. Generally, the lower the opus number the earlier the work, but not necessarily, which adds to the confusion . . . er, the fun. A youthful work might have been published late in the composer's career, after he won popularity. Or he could have disowned all his early music and made a mature piece his official Op. 1. You never know. Sometimes, the publisher issued more than one work at once—say, three piano sonatas published simultaneously—so he would christen them Op. Whatever, Nos. 1, 2 and 3. It's that simple.

Of course, not all music has an opus number. Sometimes you see "K."-something or "D."-something. And, so help me God, there's even "WoO"-something. Help! Or should I say "Aiuto!"

Hear this: "K." stands for Ludwig Köchel, the Austrian botanist who, for a lark, decided to catalog Mozart's complete works in the nineteenth century. (People seem to have had more spare time in those days. Or maybe they were just smarter. Whatever the case, they certainly didn't waste their time watching television.) He did such a good job that his terminology, with some modifications, stuck. "D" is much the same, only this time it stands for Otto Erich Deutsch, the musicologist who made sense out of Schubert's higgledy-piggledy. In both cases, K. and D. numbers are meant to be chronological. A K. number in the five hundreds means a late work; for Schubert, a D. number in the thousands has the same significance. (WoO simply means *Werke ohne Opus*, German for works without an opus number—usually odds and ends like juvenilia or works published posthumously.) But let's remember that both Mozart and Schubert died in their thirties, so "late" doesn't necessarily mean "old."

About this "late" business. You will keep seeing references to "late Beethoven." But he's been dead for years, hasn't he?

As dead as Dillinger; since 1827, to be exact. In this case, "late" refers to a phase of his career. Beethoven is divided into three parts—early, middle and late. There is, of course, some quibbling about which period begins when, but in general there is agreement. The six string quartets of Op. 18 are early, as is the *Moonlight Sonata* (Op. 27, No. 2); the famous *Appassionata Sonata* and symphonies 3 through 8 are middle period pieces; the *Ninth*, the last five string quartets plus the *Grosse Fuge*, and the last five piano sonatas are late works. A handy rule of thumb is that the more popular the piece, the greater its chances are of being a middle-period work; the more critical admiration is expressed for a piece, the greater its chances are of being late. Aside from the

Moonlight Sonata, nobody seems to care very much about early Beethoven, which sounds a little like Haydn gone amok.

I've mentioned the *Moonlight Sonata* twice. Why do pieces have nicknames? And who coins them?

Again, it's usually the publisher, sometimes taking a cue from the composer. When asked what his sonata Op. 31, No. 2 was about, Beethoven replied gruffly, "Read Shakespeare's *Tempest.*" So the *Tempest Sonata* it became.

Let's consider another piece: Schubert's *Symphony No. 9.* It's called the *Great.* Did Schubert shout, "Boy, is this great!" while he was writing it?

He may have; he could have. He certainly should have. But the real reason it's called the *Great C major Symphony* is the same reason that one of the apostles was called James the Greater and another James the Lesser—to distinguish it (in this case, by its length) from another Schubert symphony in C major, the *Symphony No. 6.* WARNING: Sometimes you will see the *Great C major* called *Symphony No. 7.* Do not be fooled; the numbering of the Schubert symphonies used to be a little screwed up. There *is* a Schubert *Seventh,* but it's in E major, and was only sketched, never finished. It is not to be confused with the *Symphony No. 8,* better known as the *Unfinished,* which for some reason Schubert deliberately never finished. To make matters worse, some scholars have taken to disregarding the sketches for the *E major symphony* completely, and have numbered the *Unfinished* as No. 7 and the *Great* as No. 8. There ought to be a law.

Don't think, by the way, that it doesn't get more complicated than this. It does. Take the Dvorak symphonies—please! The vagaries of publishing meant that for years, there were only five of them. Then the four earlier ones were added, making a total of nine (although Dvorak—say Duh-vor-shack, more or less; Czech, don't you know—went to his grave thinking that his first symphony, *The Bells of Zlonice,* was lost). We should have known—ever since Beethoven, everybody writes nine symphonies: Schubert, Bruckner, Mahler, although Bruckner wrote a *Symphony No. 0* (yes, he did) and Mahler really wrote ten or eleven symphonies, depending on whether you count *Das Lied von der Erde* as a symphony, which you should, and . . .

In any case, the symphonies of Antonin (sometimes you see it as Anton) Dvorak used to be numbered One through Five; the famous *New World Symphony* is still often called No. 5, which it used to be, instead of No. 9, which it is now. To complicate things, though, the renumbering was not a simple matter of addition. The glowing No. 1 in D major became No. 6; the dramatic No. 2 in D minor became No. 7; No. 3 in F became No. 5; No. 4 (the delightful G major) turned into No. 8; and the *New World* became No. 9. And, of course, there were new Nos. 1, 2, 3, and 4. So there you have it. Don't ask me about Bruckner. Don't even *think* about it.

Okay, Bruckner wrote nine symphonies, but later somebody decided that an early work ought to be performed, so it was given the number zero—*Die Nullte*. Then there was the so-called *Student Symphony*, which is sometimes performed, but not very often. The trouble is, Bruckner tended to revise his rather lengthy works—or, worse, others took it upon themselves to revise them for him, both while he was alive and after he was dead—so several of the symphonies exist in different versions, including editions by a man named Haas and a man named Novak. Then somebody else decided that Bruckner's first versions, no matter how long, were really better after all, so then we had the *Urtext*, which is German for "original edition." Then . . . well, you get the picture.

Luckily, it's not always this confusing. Although, come to think of it, some of Mozart's forty-one aren't really symphonies (more like overtures, really), and Haydn's one hundred and four is more a number of convenience than an accurate count, and . . .

Whoa! I guess I'm getting carried away. I hope I'm not throwing around a lot of terms you don't understand. It's a common mistake for those of us in music to assume that everyone knows what we mean when we talk about a symphony's being in C major or E major. Is there an H major? Or a Z major? And as long as we're at it, what's a symphony, and what's a sonata, and . . .

One thing at a time. Let's start with keys. I've got mine. Did you lose yours? Just kidding. I don't mean that kind of key at all. I mean the key a piece of music is "in."

Think of a tune, any tune: *Row, Row, Row Your Boat,* for example. The last note you sing ("dream") is the key the tune is in; if we're singing in the key of C major, then both "row" and "dream" are the note C. For "key" simply means (as one new scholarly tome puts it) "the quality of a musical passage that causes it to be sensed as gravitating towards a particular note, called the key note or the tonic." Or to put it another way, can you stop singing *Row Your Boat* on the word "the"? Just as you can't finish the sentence on that word, so you can't finish the musical sentence on (in this case) the fourth step of the scale (the note F). If you believe in tonality—as most people still do—then you have to go back to C to complete your thought. And that's what the concept of key is all about.

What's tonality, you ask? Tonality simply means that the piece in question has a tonal center, usually has big broad, hummable-mummable melodies and has a final note that dominates all the others and signals The End. This is as opposed to atonality, which means the piece goes &%*&$£§£$$*&!, the audience goes zzzzzzzzz, and the music ends wherever it stops. Roughly.

Remember, though, that we don't always have to sing *Row Your Boat* in C major. We can sing it in any of the twelve major keys (there are also twelve minor keys, about which more later). We can sing it in B major. Or A-flat major. Or F-sharp major. Whatever is most comfortable for our voice. This is called transposition. It's sort of like translation from one closely related language to another: same meaning, slightly different feel.

Most people think of the minor keys as the sad ones. This is only partly right. Basically, a minor key has what we call a flat third step of the scale. If we were singing *Row Your Boat* in C minor instead of C major, we would change the note on the word *boat* to be one half-step lower—that is, one adjacent note on the piano keyboard lower. (In C major, we would sing an E-flat instead of an E.) To many people, that little change sounds sad, and composers often employ the minor key for music of a serious or grave nature.

But not always. Richard Strauss's opera *Elektra* ends with a hysterical dance for the heroine (celebrating the murder of her mother and stepfather by her brother; I tell you, operas are wild stuff), which becomes so intense that she drops down dead on the spot. Yet the final chord of this highly complex score is . . . C major! Strauss tempers the effect, however, by throwing in an E-flat minor chord just before it, and that lingering sound of E-flat in our ears colors the final sonority. To get an idea of the effect, try playing a C major chord on the piano, but crunch an E-flat into the middle of it at the same time. Wow! You're beginning to think this is fun, right?

So let's keep going. We've learned about foreign words and variant editions and pop composers who rip off classical and opus numbers and Köchel numbers and why everybody writes nine symphonies and keys and, and . . . and we're really getting into this now. So you'll be fine on your own for a while.

But don't worry. I'll be here when you need me; in fact, we'll have another chat in just a little while.

One more thing before I go. You're probably wondering what cabbages and kings have got to do with the price of beans in Kansas? Just this:

Remember what Beethoven said about Shakespeare? Same goes for Lewis Carroll. We're not in Kansas any more, Toto. Welcome to Oz. Or, more precisely, Wonderland.

INTERLUDE: MOZART

Some years back, the *New Yorker* ran a cartoon that said everything you need to know about Mozart. The scene was a desolate, ruined landscape littered with the detritus of civilization and devoid of any signs of human culture: "Life Without Mozart," it was called.

What would we do without Mozart? Without Wolfgang Amadeus (as he never called himself)? Without Wolfgang Amade (as he usually signed himself)? Without Johannes Chrisostomus Amadeus

Wolfgangus Sigismundus Mozart (to give him his baptized name)? Without Amadeus?

In music, one is always being asked, "Who is your favorite composer?" The safe answer, of course, is to hedge and to say: certain works by certain composers, depending on circumstances, mood, taste, etc. But with Mozart, we may safely throw all caution to the winds: Mozart was the greatest composer who ever lived and, probably, who ever will live.

That may seem a little extreme, but with Mozart we are on safe ground. For this most dazzling of child prodigies evolved, in the all-too-brief span of just under 36 years, from boy wonder to mature genius, the master of every musical form. But mere formal mastery alone is not enough to win him the undisputed title against such heavyweights as Beethoven and Wagner. No, Mozart's achievement goes beyond that; in Mozart's hands, the late eighteenth-century sonata, symphony, and opera were infused with a depth and breadth of spirit unmatched in musical history. If Beethoven is forever communing with an unattainable Beyond, Mozart is the great humanist. He makes us all proud to be alive and his music gives our lives meaning.

Much nonsense has been written about composers, but Mozart has attracted more than his share. Just think of the images: Mozart the rococo china doll, emitting pretty little tinkles for periwigged and powdered gentry while his stage daddy Leopold beams proudly. Mozart the foul-mouthed cretin, obscenely giggling his way to immortality while more dutiful, if duller, contemporaries gnash their teeth in envy (thus *Amadeus*). Mozart the eternal child, unable to keep his checkbook balanced or his wife in check, his hand eternally out to his better-heeled buddies—a kind of divine street person ("He always needed a guiding hand," wrote his first biographer in 1793, just two years after he died). Let's set the record straight.

The way to do that is through the music. No composer can hide his soul, or lack of same; it comes out in the notes. And in Mozart's music we hear not a porcelain figurine or a babbling imbecile or a simple-minded man-child, but a man of enormous power and self-confidence, great sexual magnetism and a heart as big as the world. Listen to the swagger that opens his last symphony, called the *Jupiter*; to the seductive drive of the overture to his opera *Così fan tutte*, still the greatest sexual comedy of manners ever penned; to the ethereal perfection of the *Clarinet Concerto*, one of his last works. Listen to these, and tell me you're hearing the work of a china doll.

Mozart's reputation, it seems to me, rises and falls in inverse relation to Beethoven's. When society prizes strife and struggle, an obstinate refusal to accept the lot fate has decreed, it turns to Beethoven. When, on the other hand, it esteems class and savoir faire, elegance wedded to emotion so sublimely that it is impossible to tell where one ends and the other begins, it reaches for Mozart.

He makes an unlikely icon. Mozart was an ugly little guy—not as ugly as Beethoven, perhaps, whose looks were legendary, but homely enough nonetheless. He was very short, even at a time when the average height was only about five feet five inches for men. His face was pitted from smallpox, a common disease of the day, and had an unpleasant yellow tinge. His blue eyes bulged out of his big head and he had a large, ungainly nose. On top of everything else, he was nearsighted.

But he did have talent. At three he was finding tunes at the keyboard and before long he was faulting his elders' intonation on the violin. He could memorize a piece of music after just a single hearing, a talent that never left him. By five he was playing both the violin and the clavier, a forerunner of the modern piano, and by six he was composing. (His older sister, Nannerl, was similarly gifted, although not to the same extravagant extent.) Mozart's father, Leopold, was a noted violinist who wrote an important treatise on violin playing. He was also something of a martinet who saw in his son not only a musician of genius but a potentially lucrative source of income. The Mozarts hit the road at an early age, playing at the great courts of Europe (including the France of Marie Antoinette) and winning plaudits at every turn. Life, it seemed, would be sweet.

Suddenly, it all went wrong. A sensation-seeking society found the child far more interesting than the man and, as Mozart aged, he found it increasingly difficult to make ends meet. The precious little boy who had charmed Marie Antoinette at the French court was now just another awkward teenager. So what if he was a genius? He was yesterday's news. Things began to go wrong with his personal life, too. Mozart's beloved mother, Anna Maria, died on one road trip to Paris, when Wolfgang was in his early twenties. (Mozart's epistolary relaying of this tragedy to his father could serve as a Freudian case study. In a letter dated July 3, 1778, he tries to break the news gently: "I have very sad and distressing news to give you. . . . My dear Mother is very ill." Actually, she had died the night before, a fact Mozart admits only at the end of a rather lengthy missive that reports first on his musical activities, then announces the death of Voltaire—"that godless arch-rascal"—*then* discusses the problems of finding a suitable opera libretto, and only then gets around to the bad news that "My dear Mother is in the hands of the Almighty.")

Mozart fell in love with Aloysia Weber, one of the four daughters of a Mannheim musician, but she ditched him for another man and he wound up settling for her sister Constanze. And there was always his father, nagging him, peppering him with advice, hectoring and harassing him to make something of himself. ("The purpose of my remarks is to make you into an honorable man. Millions have not received that tremendous favor which God has bestowed upon you. What a responsibility! And what a shame if such a great genius were to founder!" he wrote, typically. The Mozarts were indefatigable correspondents.) Talk about an Oedipus complex!

Indeed, let's talk about complexes. Peter Schaffer's play, *Amadeus* picked up on one aspect of Mozart's life and made an *idée fixe* out of it: his penchant for the pungent phrase, most often in letters to his mother (yes, his mother) and to a saucy little female cousin in Augsburg, on whom he seems to have had quite a crush. American prudishness is often offended by German earthiness, especially about bodily parts and functions, but the eighteenth century had a far more freewheeling and colorful attitude toward these things than we do today. In one of his letters to his cousin, he invites her to come and see him in Munich, where "I shall then be able to pay you my respects in my own exalted person, to pat you on the arse, kiss your hand, *mit der hintern Büchse schiessen,* embrace you, quiz you up and down, pay every farthing I owe . . . and perhaps also—? Well, adieu my angel, my darling; I can scarce await your coming." That little bit in German, left untranslated in some editions of Mozart's letter, is a bit of coarse double entendre that means, roughly, farting ("firing with the gun below").

But it was Mozart's relationship with his father that was the formative experience of his life. His mother, of course, was a saint; Leopold, on the other hand, was a particularly terrifying combination of demigod and devil. When Mozart, against his father's wishes, fell in love with a girl with no money, from a family of *musicians,* no less, he was so afraid of his father's wrath that he once again broke the news in as roundabout a way as he could. "Now then, who is the object of my love?" he wrote in 1781. "Again, do not be horrified, I beg you! Not one of the Webers? Yes, one of the Webers, but not Josepha, not Sophie, but Constanze, the middle one. . . . She is not ugly, but no one could call her a beauty. Her whole beauty consists in two little black eyes and a graceful figure. She has no wit, but wholesome common sense enough to fulfill her duties as a wife and mother." Not very gallant, to be sure, but he got the point across.

Mozart's other great battle was against the Archbishop of Salzburg (his home town). It was Leopold's great ambition for his son that he find a place in the Archbishop's service: even he, one of the greatest stage papas in history, could not comprehend the scope of his genius son's ambition. But by talent and temperament, Mozart was no more suited to court livery than he was to farming. His relations with the Archbishop went from worse to worst and finally he was dismissed with a kick in the pants from Count Karl Arco, the bishop's secretary. Mozart fled to Vienna, then the musical capital of the world.

This is where the myth becomes stronger than the man. We know he was successful. He was appointed Chamber Composer to the Emperor Joseph II, at a salary of eight hundred guldens (about $2,000) a year (his predecessor, Christoph Willibald Gluck, had been getting two thousand gulden per annum). Both *The Marriage of Figaro* and *Don Giovanni* were smash hits, especially in Prague. (Of *Figaro*, the Emperor remarked, "Too beautiful for our ears.") He became renowned as a pianist, often a soloist in his own concertos. His music was much in demand; *The Magic Flute*, a kind of Broadway show of the day, was wildly popular. Probably he made a lot of money. Certainly, he spent all of it.

"I beg you to lend me until tomorrow at least a couple of hundred gulden, as my landlord in the Landstrasse has been so importunate that in order to avoid such an unpleasant incident I have had to pay him on the spot, and this has made things very awkward for me," he wrote to one of his brothers in his Masonic lodge, the generous merchant Michael Puchberg. Despite his brave report to his father, Constanze turned out to be something of a party girl, and Mozart's letters to her in various spas plead for responsible behavior. Worn out from overwork and a kidney disease, Mozart died on December 5, 1791, and was buried in a common grave in St. Mark's cemetery, Vienna. To this day, the exact location of his grave is uncertain.

(After Mozart's death, Constanze became every inch the grieving widow. With consummate cheek, she wrote to the Emperor six days after her husband died, pleading for money. "The undersigned has had the misfortune to suffer the terrible loss of her husband and to be left by him with two infant sons in circumstances closely bordering on penury and want." Yet, widowed, Constanze proved to be a shrewd businesswoman, auctioning off publication rights to Mozart's many unpublished works, yet hanging on to the manuscripts themselves. Eventually she remarried, to a Count Nissen of Denmark, and turned her life with Mozart into a kind of cottage industry. Nissen even wrote a biography of Mozart.)

In such a short life, Mozart left a huge amount of music behind. It can seem a little intimidating, sorting through all those sonatas, symphonies and operas, not to mention the songs, chamber music and ceremonial works. Yet, paradoxically, the best of Mozart is rather easy to spot. There are the four great operas: *Figaro, Così, Don Giovanni,* and *The Magic Flute* (the first three are in Italian, the last in German), and the peripheral ones, such as *The Abduction from the Seraglio* and *La Clemenza di Tito.* There are the major symphonies, including the last three, *Symphonies Nos. 39, 40,* and *41* in E-flat, G minor and C major, respectively. There are the magnificent piano concertos, including the D minor, K. 466, and the last one, in B-flat, K. 595. There is the noble *Requiem,* left uncompleted at his death and finished by his pupil, Sussmayr, and the more festive choral works such as the *Coronation Mass.*

My recommendation is to start with the symphonies and concertos, then progress to the much longer operas. The rise of the early music movement in Britain and the United States has been a tremendous boon to Mozart performance, scraping away the layers of romantic residue that have tarnished and obscured his vision. Playing on eighteenth century strings and winds, groups such as the Academy of Ancient Music in England have revealed the vibrancy and freshness of the classical period; after hearing Christopher Hogwood lead the Academy in the Mozart symphonies, you won't want to hear them played any other way.

You won't be sorry. Discovering Mozart will change your life, disclosing hitherto unsuspected vistas of emotion and meaning in music. For beneath the periwigged visage, the quick and ready smile, and the playful sense of humor beat the heart of a man who knew both life's triumphs and its tragedies. "Before God, and as a honest man, I tell you that your son is the greatest composer known to me, either in person or by name." No less a personage than Franz Joseph Haydn said that, to Leopold Mozart.

Can we say any less?

2

WHOSE ART IS IT, ANYWAY?

A PERSONAL ODYSSEY

T he first thing to forget about classical music is its name. "Classical music" not only sounds faintly twee, it is also misleading and inaccurate. Properly speaking, the term refers only to that music written during the so-called classical period, roughly the second half of the eighteenth century, or Haydn and Mozart to you. In musical circles, it has a very specific meaning, one that is not generally shared by the world at large. Despite efforts to substitute "art music," "concert music," "serious music," or, worst of all, "good music," "classical music" has attached itself like a barnacle to the great body of musical art that ranges from the plainchant of the Middle Ages and the polyphonic motets of the Renaissance up through the neo-minimalism of today. What, really, do Josquin des Prés, Bach, Schubert, Schoenberg, and Steve Reich have in common?

The answer is both not much and a lot, which may explain the persistence of the name. Correctly, the public has always perceived some kinds of music to be more serious in intent than others— "classic," if you will—and naturally lumps it all together under a convenient rubric. In our day of bite-sized attention spans and *USA Today* factoids, there is something admirable, if a little square, about people who are still lining up to hear something composed two or three hundred years ago. Talk about golden oldies. (I mean the pieces, not the people.)

And that's the point. Classical music, or whatever you want to call it (I'll be using various names for it during the course of this book, for the sake of variety), has been around a long time because it is something of continuing cultural value, even in our multicultural (or acultural, as you like) society. After all, what is more multicultural than music? True, the great bulk of classical music was composed by white, western Europeans, but then white, western Europeans invented English, too, a language that is now spoken as a primary tongue in such disparate countries (and continents) as the United States, Australia, India, and Liberia, and which has become the world's lingua franca in trade and commerce. Anyone who has ever spent much time overseas has noticed that when an Italian from London, a Greek from the United States, a Chinese from Singapore, and a black African from Johannesburg meet, chances are they will speak to each other in . . . English.

So it is with classical music. Like English, it has spread across the world, taking root in the most ostensibly foreign of climes. In Japan, Western classical music is extremely popular; in Tokyo alone there are more than a dozen symphony orchestras and visiting Western musicians always draw large, rapt audiences. In China, brave artists kept the Western musical tradition alive through the darkest and most dangerous days of the Great Cultural Revolution; now, once again, Western-style classical music is flourishing in the People's Republic. From Bombay has come conductor Zubin Mehta; from Paris, the Chinese-American cellist Yo Yo Ma; from Korea, the violinist Kyung-Wha Chung and her brother, conductor Myung-Whun Chung. And, of course, many well-known performers have come from Japan, including conductor Seiji Ozawa and the sensational young violinist Mi Dori. Closer to home, there have been many well-known black classical performers, such as soprano Leontyne Price (who grew up in the rural South), bass Simon Estes (from Iowa), and conductor James de Priest (Philadelphia). The charge that classical music is an elitist urban entertainment suited only to the white moneyed class is hereby rejected.

Nor is a taste for classical music something you are born with, or at least into. Each of us comes to music in our own way, but some of us have further to come. Take my case, for example. My father was a military officer whose taste in music ran to country and western songs, Burl Ives, and the bagpipes; neither of my parents played a musical instrument, unless you count the harmonica; I grew up in southern California and Hawaii, in those days hardly cultural hotspots to rival New York. Yet my mother, good lace-curtain Irish lady that she is, insisted that all five of her children take piano lessons and after a while I discovered that I was pretty good at it. (So was my younger brother, who became an accomplished pianist, trombone player, recorder player, and, finally, officer in the U.S. Navy. No one says you have to make a profession out of it.)

One day, when I was in the third or fourth grade, my class was bused downtown to hear the San Diego Symphony play a children's concert. One encounter with the *Nutcracker Suite* and I was hooked forever, seduced by the sinuosity of the celesta in the "Dance of the Sugar-Plum Fairy," and thrilled by the delirious whirl of the strings in the "Waltz of the Flowers." I went home and asked my parents to buy me some records, and a bang-up version of von Suppe's *Light Cavalry Overture* (what else would we have had in our house?) soon became one of my favorite treasures.

Still, I did not really begin to get serious about serious music until I was thirteen or so. At that time, I was, for some reason, greatly enamored of big band music, and especially of the Benny Goodman bands of the mid-1930s. I loved the stuff: the crispness of the ensemble playing, the snap of Gene Krupa's drums, the fire of trumpeter Harry James, Teddy Wilson's elegant pianism, Lionel Hampton's vibrant sass.

This rather odd taste (the year was, after all, 1963 and the Beatles were soon to arrive on these shores) led me to the wider world of modern jazz—of Miles and Trane—and then, inevitably, to the fringes of concert repertory, where I stumbled upon Rimsky-Korsakov's *Scheherezade*. Once again, I was bewitched, this time not only by the force and beauty of the music, but also by its power to evoke fantastic images. Of course, I was also encountering the primal power of rock-and-roll in its second great period; the same year I found Rimsky, I also found the Beatles. And to me, there wasn't that much difference between them in quality.

There, I've said it. *Not much difference in quality.* If there is a guiding philosophy behind this book, it is the catholicity of the musical experience—and thus its universality. For musical truth and beauty are to be found in the unlikeliest venues, from the embroidered chanting of the fishermen of the Aran Islands to the densest twelve-tone passage in Pierre Boulez. My own musical world comprises both these musics, and many others as well: The Who (*Tommy*) and the Kinks (*Lola vs. Powerman and the Underground*); Andrew Lloyd Webber's *Evita;* the Tim Rice-ABBA musical, *Chess;* Morton Subotnick's all-electronic *Golden Apples of the Sun;* Philip Glass's *Satyagraha;* and John Adams's *Nixon in China*—all in addition to the standard concert repertory that runs from Bach through Mahler and Stravinsky. "There are many rooms in my Father's house," said Jesus, to which the contemporary music lover, with a world of music undreamed of by earlier generations available to him or her at the touch of a CD player, can only answer: Amen.

Back in 1969, right at the end of the Beatles' era, the American music critic Henry Pleasants published another in his series of books (*The Agony of Modern Music, Death of a Music?*) questioning whether "classical music"—or "serious music," as Pleasants contemptuously called it—was in decline. (The answer was yes.) Pleasants, as usual, got right to the heart of the matter:

Beyond, or beneath, all these more or less musical considerations, obtuse and muddled as they may be, lies a more fundamental incompatibility. Serious music is dignified. It is the symphony orchestra, opera in foreign languages, sonatas and concertos and string quartets, solemnly executed by solemn gentlemen from the universities and from Budapest and Amsterdam and Vienna and Paris. It is white tie and tails and Miss This and Mr. That and Madame So-and-so—and Maestro! It is a survivor of an Old World that is expiring rapidly, even in the Old World.

Right on, Henry. If you, like me, are a member of the Baby Boom generation, then chances are you grew up listening to rock-and-roll, whether you wanted to or not. You couldn't help it. It was on the radio, and who among us can say he or she was too cool to have (or have wanted) a transistor radio back in the early sixties. Rock was a generational talisman, something that set us apart from our parents during this most rebellious of rebellious ages. If they hated rock, so much the better! To us, rock music was not an alien encroachment on the divine harmony of Mozart, but a vital musical idiom that spoke our language at a time when nothing else did.

My point here is not that Frankie Valle and the Four Seasons are necessarily the equal of Verdi, or even Frank Sinatra. There was much amusement when, in the first flush of Beatlemania, learned musicologists in Britain wrote exegeses comparing the Fab Four's gift for songwriting to Schubert's. It seemed then like so much academic overkill, a pathetic attempt by aging professors—they must have been all of forty years old—to grab hold of the youthful bandwagon before it left them forever in the dust. Much as I admired the Beatles—and they were, without a doubt, the best and most influential rock band of the sixties—I didn't think at the time that they were the equal of Schubert.

But twenty years later, I'm not as sure as I once was. There do seem to be some striking similarities. Schubert died a couple of months short of his thirty-second birthday; the Beatles broke up when they were even younger. Both were master songwriters with a sure sense of structure and a gift for the disarming melodic turn of phrase, which is different from a mere gift for melody. Both had an ear for the unexpected, piquant harmony. And both set their native language (German, in the Austrian Schubert's case; English, in the Anglo-Irish Beatles') in masterly fashion. Maybe those musicologists were on to something after all.

So, then, how do we decide which is better? Wait. The fact that we are even making this choice says something about our aesthetics. *Art music and classical music are not necessarily the same thing.* That is, while art music comprises the whole of classical music, classical music is not coterminous with art music. Now it is time for you to be exposed to a vastly larger storehouse of musical wealth, one that (as the cliché has it) has stood the test of time. It is a world in which many of the choices have already been made for you—the standard repertory—but one which also amply repays any exploration you do yourself.

Okay, I can hear your question now: what is this repertoire—or repertory—stuff, anyway?

A fancy French word, sometimes anglicized as "repertory," repertoire refers to those works that are commonly played by musicians the world over. Generally speaking, the standard symphonic repertoire runs from Bach through Stravinsky and Schoenberg. In practice, though, it is a little narrower, beginning with Haydn and Mozart and ending with Mahler and early Stravinsky—about 120 years of musical history. In between come such luminaries as Beethoven, Schubert, Chopin, Schumann, Liszt, Berlioz, Wagner, Brahms, and Bruckner and Richard Strauss. The operatic repertory is much the same. Mozart's great works mark one pole, while Puccini's delineate the other—that is, from 1780 to 1925. Chamber music, music's third great branch, ranges a little further afield, from the trios of Haydn through the quartets of Bela Bartok. When you say the word *repertoire*, you're talking about pieces that everybody knows, or should.

When we talk about the symphonic repertoire, we mean music that was written to be played by a symphony orchestra. That is, by an ensemble of 50 or more players, ranging as high as 110. The symphony orchestra—there is undoubtedly one in your town—is a fundamentally romantic concept. Now by "romantic" I don't mean a bodice-ripper novel about love on the Scottish heaths and cliffs. No, "romantic" refers to the artist movement that swept Europe in the late eighteenth and early nineteenth centuries, first in the pictorial arts and literature (the paintings of Caspar David Friedrich, for example, or the poetry of Goethe), and later in music (some of Beethoven, most of Schubert, all of Chopin and Liszt). Romanticism may no longer be in fashion, creatively speaking, having long ago been superseded in music by serialism (Schoenberg's "method of composing with the twelve tones," about which more later) and minimalism (the works of Philip Glass, Steve

Reich, and John Adams—see the Interlude on modern American music elsewhere in this book). Audiences, however, have never given up on it, and to this day romantic music remains far and away the most popular music in the repertoire. Which would you rather hear: the Tchaikovsky *Pathetique* or Anton Webern's *Symphony*?

So, symphonically speaking, what are we talking about for beginners? A handful of symphonies by Mozart and Haydn, Beethoven's famous nine, one or two by Schubert, Berlioz's *Symphonie Fantastique*, four by Brahms, three of Tchaikovsky's six, and a couple by Mahler. That's the repertoire. Not so bad, is it? You are the guy who can hum the theme songs from *Rawhide* and *The Flintstones* without having looked at the music for thirty years, the woman who knows the lyrics to every Top Forty song of the sixties. Is it really so tough to learn a few symphonies?

Or a few operas. (Wait, don't go! At least stick around until Chapter Four.) Granted, operas are longer than symphonies—sometimes a lot longer—but they generally have fun, if highly improbable, stories attached to them, and there is plenty to look at as well. What's more, you can get away with knowing even fewer operas than symphonies: four by Mozart, one by Beethoven, four or five by Verdi, one by Bizet, a couple by Wagner, two or three by Puccini and a couple by Richard (no kin to Johann the Waltz King) Strauss. I'm going to insist that you add Berg's *Wozzeck* and Shostakovich's *Lady Macbeth of Mtzensk* to this list and some day, believe me, you will thank me for it.

In chamber music, long considered the most recondite of classical music's manifestations, we can start slowly, with a few Beethoven string quartets, Schubert's irresistible *Trout Quintet* and his *C major string Quintet*, the Brahms *Piano Quintet*, the Dvorak *Dumky Trio*, the Debussy and Ravel string quartets and the *Piano Trio* by Charles Ives. Chamber music has the reputation of being the ultimate egghead pursuit, but you will soon discover that the smaller the number of instruments, the more sublime and elegant the musical message.

We next venture into the mysterious world of choral music. Actually, it's not so mysterious at all. Remember the play, *Anybody*

Can Whistle? Anybody can sing, too. (Well, almost anybody.) And with a little coaching almost everyone can sing choral music. (The San Francisco Symphony, for example, offers an annual sing-along *Messiah.*) It's the ultimate audience-participation music.

The problem is, choral music is better in some nations than in others. The British, for example, have a highly developed choral tradition and for hundreds of years, British composers have been churning out works to meet the demand of choral societies all across the country: Sir Hubert Parry, Charles Villiers Stanford—names you don't want to know—as well as Sir Edward Elgar, Gustav Holst, and Ralph Vaughan Williams, which are names you do. Germany, too, revels in a choral tradition (the Germans and the English are, after all, cousins), which extends at least back to Bach. The choral repertoire, therefore, comes largely from these two lands. Personally, I find choral music something of an acquired taste, although there are many pieces I admire. Mozart's masses and the *Requiem;* Elgar's masterpiece, *The Dream of Gerontius;* Vaughan Williams's *A Sea Symphony;* Handel's *Messiah.* Then, too, there is the Verdi *Requiem,* a sort of grand opera in disguise, and Carl Orff's *Carmina Burana* and *Catulli Carmina,* rude, crude and sometimes lewd setting of verse by medieval monks and poetry of ancient Rome.

And then, most terrifying of all, there are art songs—the dreaded *lieder* (pronounced "leader"), which is nothing more than the German word for *songs.* But these are actually the simplest musical forms of all, and closest in intent to the rock songs you grew up with: songs of love and death. When gathered together into what we call cycles, they form small morality plays that are among music's most moving creations. Take your girlfriend to a performance of Robert Schumann's sentimental *Frauenliebe und -Leben* (Woman's Love and Life), follow along with a good translation and, I guarantee, she'll be yours forever. You see, there are practical applications of your new knowledge as well.

So much for the repertoire stuff. As we go, we'll be discussing pieces by name, and before you know it, you'll be building a repertoire yourself. The easy way.

For me, in the wilds of Hawaii and, later, in the culturally disadvantaged suburbs of Washington, D.C., my unguided exploration of the repertory resulted in many false steps along the way. In high school in Honolulu, I formed a jazz trio with a clarinetist and a drummer (I was on piano), and we had a devil of a time trying to play written music together until we finally figured out that the clarinet sounds a note lower than its music is written: that is, a written "C" will sound on the clarinet as "B-flat." Don't ask why.

Some hit-or-miss purchases by my mother put a few classical anthologies in my growing record collection; one exciting addition to my library was Stravinsky conducting his three great ballets, *The Firebird, Petrouchka,* and *The Rite of Spring.* Much later, I discovered that Stravinsky the conductor was basically a fraud. His performances often were rehearsed by his Boswell, Robert Craft, and only led by the old man at the performance. No matter. My appetite was whetted and soon my piano lessons were not enough to slake my thirst for more. I raided the libraries for books about music and recordings; I read everything I could, including *High Fidelity* and *Stereo Review.* I also stumbled on Harold C. Schonberg's books, including *The Great Pianists.* Schonberg's clear, lucid readability fired my imagination; little did I suspect back then that someday the senior music critic of the New York *Times* would become my mentor and friend.

Inevitably, my autodidacticism sometimes led me astray. Take the string quartet. The first example of this sublime art form that I descried was the scherzo movement of Claude Debussy's delicious *String Quartet* (he wrote only one). This is an amazing piece, played by the four instruments—two violins, viola, and cello— mostly pizzicato; that is, with the strings'plucked, not bowed. Like the blind man who felt the elephant's leg and deduced it to be a tree, I leaped to the erroneous conclusion that *all* string quartets must be like this and promptly ran headlong into the late Beethoven quartets. Needless to say, the late quartets of Beethoven—that is, the five quartets the composer wrote near the end of his life, when he was at his most complex and visionary— bear about as much resemblance to Debussy's refined turn-of-the-century French aesthetic as a Gothic cathedral does to a salon. My premature encounter with the *Heiliger Dankgesang* scared me off the Beethoven quartets for years.

The point is, classical music does require a certain level of sophistication on the part of the listener before it gives up all its secrets. At 15, I was simply not ready for late Beethoven; nor is it likely that you are right now, either, no matter what your age. But I got there, and so will you. (In the next chapter, we'll talk about exactly how to go about listening to a piece of music.)

Despite my self-administered musical education, I was accepted at the Eastman School of Music in Rochester, N.Y., and joined the freshman class in the fall of 1967. Among my teachers over the next four years were the late Charles Warren Fox, the eminent American musicologist, and my literature teacher, Alice Bensten, who acquainted me with everyone from Thomas Mann to Hannah Arendt. My two German teachers, Alexander Wieber and Jessie Kneisel, introduced me to the language and poetry of central Europe.

In a city whose normal winter temperature was a good 60 degrees colder than what I had been used to, the biggest shock was the degree of cultivation of some of my classmates—New York City kids, who had grown up in Carnegie Hall, who had heard Horowitz's great comeback recital in 1965, who had attended the High School of Music and Art uptown, who knew what solfege and hemiola and root position were. My good friend Joseph Packales was the son of a garment district manufacturer of women's coats who had lost first his fortune and then his health, and died while Joe was a student. Two years ahead of me, Joe was the most talented musician in the school: a splendid and sensitive pianist, adept at theory, and a fine composer who has gone on to a successful career in academe. As college students will, we spent many long hours discussing music far into the night. It was Joe who introduced me to the bulk of the repertoire, never making fun of my ignorance of such fundamentals as *La Boheme* and *Winterreise*, but always urging me, the *goyishe* brat from nowhere, on to new discoveries.

The point I'm trying to make with all this personal history is that classical music is for everyone. Surely, my own military upbringing was hardly conducive to a love for classical music; is there anyone more amusical than a Marine Corps colonel? Nor were the places where I lived as a boy and as a young man cultural hotbeds; in the 1950s, San Diego was best regarded as a great town to get a tattoo in, and Honolulu still is viewed as an island paradise best suited to working on one's tan away from the tense, hectic, pressured environment of southern California.

No, to love classical music you need not to have grown up within walking distance of Lincoln Center or Carnegie Hall. Your parents needn't have been doctors, psychiatrists or the editors of major newspaper cultural sections. It is not necessary for you to have been a prodigy on the piano, violin or cello, nor do you even need to have played clarinet in the local high school band. All the above may help, of course, but in the end, it is more nature than nurture that will lead you to music and keep you there. The discovery of classical music can be one of the transforming moments of your life, revealing a hitherto unknown world of intellectual challenge and emotional pleasure.

So let's get ready. Turn off the television; if you've seen one episode of *Moonlighting* or *thirtysomething*, you've seen them all. Forget about table envy at your local power restaurant; for the price of dinner for two these days, you can buy three or four decent seats at the Met. Don't worry about the movies: that's what you got the VCR for, wasn't it? Get to the gym in the morning or at lunchtime (you don't need to eat a big expense account lunch five days a week, anyway). And by the time most concerts begin, the children should be in bed. If they're not, they're old enough for you to take them with you.

As you start along the road to musical sophistication—the *gradus ad Parnassum*—all you really need is desire; exposure will surely follow. To become a connoisseur, all you need is time. If you don't have it, make it. You can do it. I know you can.

Whose art is it, anyway? Yours, mine—and ours.

INTERLUDE: BEETHOVEN

If there is one composer who personifies classical music for millions of listeners all over the world, that composer is Ludwig van Beethoven. The disheveled, gruff-mannered, hot-tempered Beethoven is the archetypal man of genius locked in mortal combat with the gods. In his youth he was the greatest of piano virtuosos, an elemental performer who could pound the puny instruments of his day into matchsticks. Stricken by a progressive, incurable deafness—just as he was finding his stride as a composer—he contemplated killing himself in one of the most famous, poignant suicide notes ever written, then defied the fates to write music of unprecedented breadth and stunning imaginative sweep that challenged performers and audiences alike with its fierce, uncompromising integrity. By his death in 1827 Beethoven had become transformed into the Artist as Hero, and his funeral in Vienna brought more than ten thousand people into the streets to pay him homage.

If anything, Beethoven is even more celebrated today. His nine symphonies, five piano concertos, thirty-two piano sonatas and sixteen string quartets are the touchstones of the repertoire; if you haven't really made it until you've played Carnegie Hall, then you haven't made it even there until you have played Beethoven. Chamber groups gear up for cycles of the string quartets, pianists gird their loins to do battle with the *Emperor Concerto* and the *Hammerklavier Sonata*, while conductors and orchestras the world over routinely test their mettle with the symphonies. The composer's appeal is universal: in Japan, where Beethoven is revered, there are so many performances of his *Ninth Symphony* at the end of each year that the annual eruption is known as "*Ninth* pollution." And let us not forget that it was the *Ninth* of "Ludwig van," with its exuberant setting of Schiller's *Ode to Joy*, that was the only thing even temporarily capable of soothing the brutal savage breast of Alex the Droogie in *A Clockwork Orange*.

Surely the creator of some of the world's most sublime music was himself a man of rare taste and refinement. But if there has ever been a greater disparity between a man and artist, it is hard to imagine. Physically, Beethoven was far from the heroic ideal: short (about five feet four inches), bulky, wild-haired, with prominent teeth and a dark, swarthy complexion that gave rise to his youthful nickname of The Spaniard. His life was chaotic, a succession of failed love affairs, family quarrels, heated lawsuits, ruined lodgings, cheated publishers, offended patrons, strained friendships. A visitor to one of Beethoven's flats in 1809 left this account of the composer's surroundings:

Picture to yourself the darkest, most disorderly place imaginable—blotches of moisture covered the ceiling; an oldish grand piano, on which the dust disputed the place with various pieces of engraved and manuscript music; under the piano (I do not exaggerate) an unemptied chamber pot. . . . The chairs, mostly cane-seated, were covered with plates bearing the remains of last night's supper. . . .

The chamber pot under the piano is a nice touch. With one important exception—his nephew Karl, with whom he had a tumultuous, ultimately unhappy relationship—nothing much mattered to the prickly Beethoven but his music. If musicians like Haydn and Mozart had been content to use the servants' entrance in their dealings with their royal patrons, Beethoven bulled his way in the front door. When Napoleon crowned himself emperor, Beethoven indignantly tore up the inscription of his third symphony to the little Corsican and dedicated the work instead to the "memory of a great man." His philosophy was strongly personal— "strength is the morality of the man who stands out from the rest, and it is mine," he said. If he had a notion of universal brotherhood, of the triumph of man unfettered by arbitrary context of birth or position—still, Beethoven was never a man of the masses. His were the solitary convictions of the artist who creates his own truth. "What is in my heart must come out and so I write it down," he said simply.

This towering figure was born into unprepossessing circumstances. The Beethoven family was of Belgian origin (thus "van," not "von"). Ludwig's paternal grandfather was an excellent basso whose career brought him to the provincial Rhineland city of Bonn in 1733, where he eventually rose to become *Kapellmeister* of the local court. Beethoven's father, Johann, however, was downwardly mobile, marrying the cook's daughter and scraping by as a voice, piano, and violin teacher to support his wife and three sons. With the example of Mozart fresh in memory, Johann mercilessly drove his talented son Ludwig, shaving a couple of years off his age to make him appear more prodigious. The earliest account of Beethoven's talents appeared in 1783 in a German musical magazine. Noting incorrectly that he was "a boy of eleven years"—actually, he was over twelve— and a "most promising talent," the notice continued:

He plays the piano very skillfully and with power, reads at sight very well and I need say no more than that the chief piece he plays is The Well Tempered Clavier *of Sebastian Bach. . . . This youthful genius is deserving of help to enable him to travel. He would surely become a second Wolfgang Amadeus Mozart if he were to continue as he has begun.*

Not for Beethoven, however, would be Mozart's frustrating quest for a court position after his years as a child star were over. Or Mozart's graceful, fluid style of pianism. Shortly after achieving his majority, Beethoven headed for Vienna, the musical capital of the world, where he promptly set the populace on its ear with his ferocious brand of string-busting piano playing. The refined, fragile pianos of the late eighteenth century were a far cry from their modern descendants, and it can be argued that Beethoven was in part responsible for the mechanical improvements that ultimately resulted in the steel-stringed behemoths we know today. An unparalleled improviser who could hold audiences spellbound for hours, Beethoven quickly established himself as the angry young man of his profession. Oddly, this young Turk, this blatant revolutionary, was almost immediately taken to heart by the aristocracy. When Beethoven was offered a remunerative position in Westphalia, Archduke Rudolf, Prince Lobkowitz, and Prince Kinsky quickly raised a handsome annuity to keep him in Vienna. Beethoven, however, always maintained his self-esteem. The story goes that once he and the great German poet, Johann Wolfgang von Goethe, were walking together when a member of the nobility passed by. Goethe doffed his hat in respect and stood aside, but Beethoven kept on going. "My nobility," he said on another occasion, pointing to his head and his heart, "is *here* and *here*."

This formidable, irascible man never married, although at one time Beethoven seems to have seriously considered it. Perhaps because they were impossibly beyond his reach, Beethoven time and again fell in love with women, some of them married, of a higher social class: the Countess Giulietta Guicciardi, Josephine von Brunswick, Therese Malfatti, Bettina Brentano, Antonie Brentano (Bettina's sister-in-law), Dorothea von Ertmann, to name a few. Indeed, in the summer of 1812 Beethoven wrote an ardent letter to an unnamed "immortal beloved," in which he invoked "my angel, my all, my very self . . . can you change the fact that you are not wholly mine, I not wholly thine. . . ." This letter followed by a decade the equally passionate Heiligenstadt Testament, written in a village outside Vienna, addressed to his brothers and intended to be read after his death. Crushed by his deafness and contemplating his own self-destruction—and this before he had even written the *Eroica* Symphony—Beethoven wrote in 1802: "Oh you who think or say that I am malevolent, stubborn or misanthropic, how greatly do you wrong me." Who among us, faced with the loss of our livelihood, could have maintained our composure any better?

Like Janus, Beethoven stands at a turning point in musical history, at once facing back to the classical period and forward to romanticism. And like both Caesar's Gaul and a New York Rangers hockey game, Beethoven's life's work is divided into three parts, early, middle and late. As a young barn-burner in Vienna, Beethoven had a rather adversarial relationship with his teacher, Haydn. This unlikely pedagogical relationship was doomed to fail, for reasons of temperament if nothing else, but from Haydn Beethoven learned both classic form and, more important, how to channel his expression, to give it controlled voice. Beethoven's *First Symphony*, for example, at once proclaims Haydn's influence even as it rejects it: ostensibly in C major, the symphony begins audaciously in F before quickly modulating to the home key, something no classical-period composer in his right mind would ever dream of doing. In the *Second Symphony*, the shaggiest of Beethoven's essays in the form, Haydn's bumptious high spirits can be heard in the first movement's extravagant coda (the word means "tail" in Italian, and refers to a concluding section that is really a kind of afterthought). The six early string quartets of Op. 18, too, bear Haydn's fingerprints; what they lack in the older man's consummate sophistication, they make up for in sheer rude energy. And the first two piano concertos have a classicism about them that is unmistakably eighteenth century in feel.

Suddenly, it all changed. About the time that his deafness became nearly total, Beethoven's style underwent a metamorphosis, exploding the boundaries of the classical forms bequeathed to him, to venture into territory where no composer had gone before. "I will seize Fate by the throat; it shall certainly not crush me completely. . . ." In works such as the *Eroica, Fifth, Seventh* and *Ninth* symphonies; piano sonatas such as the *Appassionata;* his only opera, *Fidelio;* and the late string quartets, Beethoven chose to fight, throwing down the gauntlet and declaring that he would never surrender to his disability. In his hands, the classical forms were vastly enlarged in scope; the *Eroica,* for example, is twice as long as any symphony had ever been, featuring a huge opening movement; a funeral march of unprecedented depth of expression; a boisterous scherzo; and a finale that takes an innocuous theme from Beethoven's earlier *Creatures of Prometheus* ballet and transforms it into a theme and variation movement that is an emotional tour de force.

This is Beethoven the heaven-stormer, the thunderer, the fate-seizer, the Beethoven we know best and love most. He echoes down the nineteenth century. It was he who paved the way for the expansive symphonies of his contemporary Schubert, and his spiritual descendants Mahler and Bruckner (almost every Bruckner symphony begins with a string tremolo, a tip of the hat to Beethoven's *Ninth*). Brahms, who was haunted by him all his life, held off writing his first symphony for years, fearful it would be compared by his well-wishers to Beethoven's great works in the form. And it was Beethoven who struck the young Richard Wagner with the force of a thunderclap and inspired (again with the *Ninth*, perhaps the most seminal work in musical romanticism) Wagner's concept of the *Gesamtkunstwerk*—a forbidding-looking German word that simply means an all-encompassing work of art.

The one work that best demonstrates this duality, this transformation from classicist to romanticist, is the opera *Fidelio*. Always a hard worker—Beethoven would write and rewrite until he got it just right—Beethoven worked especially hard at what for him was an uncongenial medium. Originally called *Leonore, Fidelio* underwent several revisions before achieving its final form. Even so, its evolution from simple farcical *singspiel*—something akin to musical comedy, with spoken dialogue in German—to an opera of elemental force is writ large. The heroine, Leonore, has disguised herself as a man and taken a job in a prison in order to free her wrongfully imprisoned husband, Florestan. Naturally, the jailer's daughter falls in love with her, and the beginning of the opera contains several light character arias that give almost no hint of the drama to come. But the opera turns darkly serious with the introduction of the villain, Pizzaro, and by the time we finally see Florestan in the gloomy durance of his dungeon vile, we are in deep waters indeed. Leonore's quest is one of the most stirring in all opera, an impassioned plea for freedom and justice that is revolutionary in its fervor.

Yet there is another, less remarked side to Beethoven. This fearsome man could be gentle and lyrical, as in the *G major String Quartet* of Op. 18, No. 2, and the slow movements of the *Pathetique* and *Moonlight* sonatas. He could even be downright unbuttoned, as in the bucolic *Pastorale* and frisky *Eighth* symphonies. In Beethoven's music lies a world of bitter experience, of heartache, and of exhilarating, electric victory. It is a cry from the heart, a shout of triumph, an ode to joy. He is a composer for all moods, all tastes, all seasons.

3

THINGS THAT GO BUMP IN THE NIGHT

HOW TO LISTEN TO A

CONCERT OR OPERA

I know, I know. You're scared.

Scared of going to a concert, that is. It's all very well for me to talk about Wonderland, but to you a concert hall is more like a haunted house. Beethoven! Schoenberg! Boo!

What's the problem? Hundreds of thousands of people—some of them no smarter than you!—go to concerts every day. Yet you, like some Tin Woodsman (I don't want to hear about your tin ear), stand around and wonder what they've got that you don't. The answer is: courage. (I guess it was the Cowardly Lion I was really thinking of. No matter.)

How do you listen to a piece of classical music? Obviously, the simple answer is: with your ears. But when you see everyone sitting back in their seats, lost in rapture while listening to Mahler in the middle of one of his most dilatory circumlocutions, then to you it all seems confusing. And long, of course. Very, very long. What are you supposed to think about? What if you get bored? What if you've finished reading the program notes and you're down to the ads? What if you fall asleep? This is what really terrifies you.

Don't worry; be happy. This is the hard part. The easy part, too.

In the minds of laypeople, one of the most intimidating things about classical music is the simple act of hearing it. Classical aficionados, the thinking goes, know how to listen better than the rest of us, thanks to some mysterious God-given talent. They must have the aural keys in their possession that permit them to unlock the baffling structure of a sonata allegro and feast on the emotional content that lies within. Sort of like cracking a coconut. Easy and rewarding if you know how, difficult and frustrating if you don't.

Now, I'm not going to pretend that listening to *Erwartung* by Arnold Schoenberg is the easiest thing in the world. Or that *Wozzeck* and *Lulu* are laugh riots. Or even that something more basic and accessible, such as a Beethoven symphony, is a piece of cake. Listening to music is an active undertaking, not a passive one. Yes, some people do fall asleep at a concert, and it's not always their fault, either; it might be that the performance is just another routine exposition of a familiar masterpiece that offers no food for thought. (Warning: there are a lot of those.) But I guarantee you that if you're at a memorable concert and paying attention, there is no way you will embarrass yourself.

Just promise me one thing, though. Don't clap. Between movements, that is. And after the performance, too. Until you hear many, many others around you clapping. Then you can join in.

What's wrong with clapping, you wonder? Not a thing. Happens all the time. Time was when folks clapped whenever they felt like it. Composers loved it, because it meant they had a hit on their hands. In the eighteenth and nineteenth centuries, in fact, enough applause and the next thing you knew the piece was being performed again. That's what "Encore!" really means: Play it again, Sam (or Lenny). Nowadays an encore is another piece that the performer just so happens to have prepared for just this occasion. But in the old days, they just played the tune over again. And over. And sometimes over.

And now? Now we're much more decorous. It's not a bad idea. Usually, we're listening to a piece we've all (or most of us) heard many times before. (In one sense, 95 percent of our concert life is an encore.) The reason we don't clap between movements in a symphony or a concerto is to maintain the integrity of the piece, to allow our fellow patrons to keep their attention focused on the grand sweep of the composer's argument. It's a form of politeness that is well observed.

My other point is to be sure the piece is really over before you start to clap. Sometimes composers are sneaky, and they throw in false endings just to see who's paying attention. One of the most famous false endings in music comes in the finale of Schubert's *Trout Quintet*. The music appears to come to a full stop, pauses briefly, and then repeats itself. You can always tell the tyros in the audience with this one. In fact, . . .

At a concert in Salzburg one Christmas, a group of Japanese tourists fell right into the trap, and started to applaud madly. The Austro-Germans do not take this sort of *faux pas* lightly, and the collective "Shhhhhhhhh" temporarily drowned out the music. So it's best to wait until you're absolutely sure the tune is finished. One foolproof way is to wait for the musicians to put down their instruments and stand up. Remember, no one will notice if you're the last guy to clap, but they sure will if you're the first—especially if you're wrong.

You notice I haven't said anything about opera yet. That's because in opera people do just the opposite. They clap. They cheer. They scream "Bravo!" at the top of their lungs at the least little provocation. In other words, they go crazy. Opera does that to people. (We'll talk more about opera in Chapter Four.)

But even in opera, there are some rules. Nobody interrupts a diva or a tenor in the middle of an aria (death to the infidel is the unhappy result). It's also not polite to clap while the curtain is descending at the end of an act *if the music is quiet*. A composer like Puccini expected folks to go wild at a big close—the end of Act One of *Tosca*, for instance—but preferred to maintain the dramatic tension elsewhere—the end of Act Two of *Tosca*, or the final moments of the first act of *La Boheme*. Europeans tend to observe the distinction better than Americans do.

Another thing. In opera, it's okay to boo. And people do it all the time.

Yes, they do. Going to the opera is a little bit like going to the circus (for some of the canary fanciers in the audience, it's exactly like going to the circus), or maybe a bullfight. Woe betide the hapless soprano who blows the Queen of the Night's arias in *The Magic Flute*, or the Verdi heroine without the proper fire in her belly. Not only singers get booed, either. It's very popular these days to boo the conductor, the stage director, the scenic designer, even sometimes the lighting guy. Opera's not for the squeamish. You're beginning to get the picture, as far as decorum is concerned. But let's get back to the subject. How do you listen? The key to understanding classical music is that it has a structure. Every good piece of music does. When you listen to a rock song, you're listening to a structure. You know: verse, chorus, break, verse, chorus, end. (Roy Orbison's *Only the Lonely*—which just so happens to be the greatest example of bel canto singing of the twentieth century—for example.) Classical music's the same, just a little more complicated. All right, sometimes a lot more complicated.

But there are clues provided, often in the very title of a work, to help you listen. A sonata, for example, is a work for one or two instruments—usually piano or piano and violin—that follows a traditional pattern of three or four movements: fast, slow, moderate, fast, with the second fast movement usually faster than the first and the moderate movement often a dance in three-quarter time. So when we see Beethoven's *Moonlight Sonata* on the program, even if we haven't heard it before, right away we know what to expect.

The next thing to know is that each movement has its own structure. The first movement of a sonata is most often cast in what we call sonata-allegro form. (The "allegro" part refers to the tempo, for "allegro" means quick.) The classic sonata form goes like this: 1) Exposition: first theme in the main key, second theme in a closely related key; 2) Development, in which the composer puts both his tunes through their paces, sometimes changing them in ways that you have to follow closely, until he gradually leads them back to the 3) Recapitulation, in which both tunes come back, usually in the home key. Thus a sonata in C major would have its first tune in C major, its second tune in G major (the so-called "dominant"), its development in various keys, and its recap in C. The classic symphony is nothing but a sonata for orchestra. And that's all there is to it! (Well, almost.)

The main thing to remember is that the composer is not just writing down the first thing that comes into his head. Each part of his composition must relate to the others in a logical, coherent, organic way. That goes not only for individual movements, but for larger structures like complete symphonies and sonatas too. Music is a language: the themes in each movement are like complete sentences, which when combined turn into larger paragraphs, or movements. Put a few paragraphs together and the next thing you know, you've got a short story; keep going and you've got a novel. Or, in this case, a symphony.

The four movements of, say, Beethoven's *Fifth* are not just a random collection of stray tunes; you couldn't drop the second movement and substitute another Beethoven slow movement for it and still have the *Fifth Symphony*. The character would be all wrong, the keys wouldn't relate, the speed would be off, and so forth. It just wouldn't work.

Operas are much longer and more sprawling than symphonies, of course, but even they have discernible structures—which, when we examine them, turn out to be relatively simple. Arias, for example, those stop-the-opera moments when a singer stands and delivers, are often cast in the most elementary of musical forms: ABA, also known as da capo form. No, that's not a Swedish rock group, it's a form in which A stands for the first tune, B for the second, and A for the reprise of the first. Arias in the eighteenth century (Handel's operas, for example) were often da capo arias. (Another name for the ABA form is the rondo, which usually runs a little longer, thus: ABACADA. The point is, one tune keeps recurring.)

As opera evolved, some composers experimented with macro-designs. Alban Berg, for example, the great twentieth century Austrian composer, cast each of the three acts of *Wozzeck* in a large form. The first act is a suite, the second is a symphony, and the third a set of variations.

That's "variations." V-a-r-i-a-t-i-o-n-s. It's one of the simplest and oldest of musical forms, and to my mind one of the best. You take a tune, play it through straight once, then alter it in clever ways. It can be something as simple as the Beatles' *Hey Jude*, as spiritual as Ralph Vaughan Williams's *Fantasia on a Theme of*

Thomas Tallis for string orchestra, or as stirring as Sir Edward Elgar's *Enigma Variations*, or as mighty as Brahms's *Variations on a Theme of Haydn.*
   Now, what do we mean by "on a theme of"? Do composers borrow from each other? Do they steal?
   Yes and yes. They don't steal from the living as much as they used to, because there are laws against that sort of thing now. Bach stole several concertos by Vivaldi and arranged them for organ and orchestra, for example. Johann Pepusch, who arranged tunes and composed the overture for John Gay's delightful *The Beggar's Opera* in the eighteenth century, ripped off a march from Handel's *Rinaldo*—this while Handel was alive and well and living across town in London. Nobody thought much of it then.
   Now, it's better manners to acknowledge your source. In the Vaughan Williams piece mentioned above, the twentieth century English composer reached back to a sixteenth century predecessor for a conscious homage. The late Benjamin Britten honored his teacher Frank Bridge with a spectacular series of variations on a Bridge tune. Earlier, Brahms composed one of his most effective piano works on a theme of Handel (the *Variations on a Theme of Handel*) and also wrote the *Variations on a Theme of Haydn*—although in fact the tune is probably not Haydn's at all and the smart set today refers to this piece as the *Variations on the St. Antony Chorale*—in two versions, one for two pianos and one for full orchestra.
   On the other hand, some still just help themselves. Pop ripoffs of classical tunes go back at least to *Tonight We Love* (Tchaikovsky's first piano concerto) and *I'm Always Chasing Rainbows* (Chopin's *Fantasie-Impromptu*). The Toys had a hit in 1965 with a Bach tune and Eric Carmen has raided Rachmaninoff a couple of times. Mainstream classical composers today don't steal much, in part because all serial music sounds alike anyway.
   You knew we finally were going to bring up that word. Serial, I mean.
   Not cereal, serial. S-e-r-i-a-l. Twelve-tone. Dodecaphonic. (For all you twelve-tone composers in the audience, I was just kidding,

sort of.) The time has come, the walrus said, to speak of many things. . . .

Anyway, it's time to talk turkey about twelve-tone. Ready? Here's the deal (I promise I'll be brief. But you have to know this theoretical stuff if you don't want to go running out with the little old ladies whenever a tone row rears its head.)

One way to look at musical history is progressively, a teleological approach a la Teilhard de Chardin. According to this view, since the Middle Ages music has been steadily evolving toward the state of near-perfection in which it finds itself today. In so doing, it has gradually expanded the notion of what constitutes consonance, continually expanding the harmonic palette available to composers.

That's consonance. Euphony. Sounds that sound nice together. If you play a C and the G above it on the piano, for example, you have sounded a perfect fifth—the basic consonance. If you play a C and an F-sharp, you've hit a tritone—the basic extreme dissonance. Or, better yet, play a C and a C-sharp. Crunch! That's dissonance.

Slowly, then, composers began experimenting with dissonance. Hard to believe, but at one time the major third—and where would the Everly Brothers be without it?—was considered a dissonance. By the middle of the eighteenth century, though, the tonal system that we know and love was pretty much in place, a progression of tonic, subdominant and dominant chords that ultimately gave birth to rock-and-roll. In the nineteenth century, wise guys like Liszt and Wagner pushed the boundaries further, stretching the limits of tonality until, in Wagner's *Tristan und Isolde,* there are times when the listener loses all sense of a tonal center.

Wagner did this for emotional, not theoretical reasons. The delirious love that Tristan and Isolde feel for each other uproots and dislocates them from their surroundings; their lives are played out as if in a dream, and what better way to illustrate their heightened state than to have the music not only reflect it but to actively participate in it?

To the rest of the world, *Tristan* was a revelation. This was 1865, remember. There's a little bit of the anarchist in everybody—and especially Wagner, who wanted to remake the world and damn near did.

Let me back up a little. What's all this about "thirds" and "fifths" and stuff?

You knew I was going to get technical on you sooner or later. As long as you can add and subtract, it's really quite simple. Music has two tonal components, melody and harmony. Melody is a single line, one note at a time; we also call it a tune. Harmony is when two or more notes are sounded simultaneously—everything from the Everlys to the Mormon Tabernacle Choir. You can have two-note harmony, or you can have a chord (three or more notes) with all twelve tones in it. When you're the composer, it's up to you.

In the Western scale, the octave is partitioned into twelve equal degrees, called tones. This is not the only way to divide up the octave, of course. In Asia, there are five note scales; the late Harry Partch, an authentic American original, divided up the octave into hundreds of microtonal intervals, and built special instruments to play them. But ever since Bach codified the tonal system in *The Well-Tempered Clavier*, composers in Europe and America have been more or less satisfied with the fixed, twelve-note system.

Which is not to say that they wrote twelve-tone music. (You didn't think I forgot about that, did you?) Relationships between notes are measured by how far away they are from each other. Each note on the piano keyboard is one half-step from its nearest neighbor on either side, whether black or white. (Integration has long been accomplished in music, as the Stevie Wonder-Paul McCartney song *Ebony and Ivory* points out.) Two half steps make one whole step, which is called a second. On the piano keyboard, the notes C and D are a second apart, one whole step. C and E are a third, C and F a fourth, C and G a fifth, C and A a sixth, and C and B a seventh. C and C, of course, are an octave apart.

I'm not ignoring the black keys; it's just that they're a little more complicated. What about the C-sharps and the E-flats?

One particularly neat thing about intervals is that you can flip them over. If you flip the second, for example—go from D up to C—you get a seventh. Flip a third, get a sixth. Invert a fourth and you have a fifth. This principle works in both directions, by the way.

But the keyboard is not all white notes. So theorists developed the idea of quantifying the types of second, thirds and fourths by calling them major or minor. (There are also augmented and diminished intervals, but that's a little more sophisticated than we need to be.) C to D is, as we've seen, a major second. C to C-sharp (or D-flat, which is the same note on the keyboard) is a minor second. C to E is a major third; C to E-flat is a minor third. C to A is a major sixth; C to A-flat is a minor sixth. C to B is a major seventh; C to B-flat is minor.

I think you see what's coming. Right! If you reverse, or flip, a small interval, you get the opposite large interval, and vice versa. Reverse the step from C to E-flat (a minor third) and you get E-flat to C: a major sixth. Flip the major sixth of C to A—that is, make A the bottom note and C the top—and you have a minor third. That's the way intervals work.

What about fourths and fifths? You noticed I haven't spoken of minor fourth and fifths yet. In fact, a little while back, I used the word *perfect* in regard to the fifth. What's perfect about it?

Now we're getting into the realm of acoustics and physics and the overtone series, which is not really necessary. Let this suffice: instead of major and minor, we use the words perfect, augmented and diminished when we talk about fourths and fifths. An augmented fourth and a diminished fifth are the same thing—a tritone, the unstable midpoint of the octave. A perfect fourth or fifth (remember, they are inverses of each other) is just that: the fundamental building block of our whole tonal system. Which gets us back to twelve-tone music.

What the twelve-tone composers—Arnold Schoenberg and his two disciples, Alban Berg and Anton Webern—did was to postulate that all twelve tones of the scale were created equal, and that no one of them ought to dominate. No tonal pull, no key centers, no home key, nothing.

Sound pretty dumb? Not at the time. After all, history, as we've seen, seemed to be on the serialists' side. But like communism and psychiatry, serialism is a good idea in theory but a problematic one in practice. Problematic because, like those other two nineteenth century central European inventions, it is highly culture- and period-specific and has pretty much outlived its usefulness. Plus, very few except the zealots believe in the salvation power of any of them anymore: psychiatrists all say their colleagues are crazy and even the Russians seem to be punting Communism. And certainly no one believes that salvation lies through serialism any more.

Still, it was an interesting idea. Because no one tone could lord it over all the others, Schoenberg decreed that all twelve would have to be heard before any one could be repeated. He called the resulting series of notes a "tone row." Now, obviously, this would get pretty monotonous if all you could do was to repeat the same sequence of twelve notes over and over, so three variants of the basic row were developed. First there was the retrograde—playing the row backward. Then there was the inversion—flipping the intervals between the tones, just as we did above. And finally there was the retrograde inversion—playing the inversion backward.

So if your row went from C to E to F in the original, in the retrograde it would go from F to E to C; in the inversion from C to A-flat to G; and in the retrograde inversion from G to A-flat to C. That's just three notes, of course, for illustration. In reality, there would be twelve.

Why would anyone want to write music like this, you wonder? It seems so cold-blooded. The problem with you is that you want all composers to be as heart-on-sleeve as Tchaikovsky. So does nearly everybody. But it would be a very dull world if all music sounded like *Tonight We Love*. I can name several twelve-tone pieces you could listen to—and like. Schoenberg's *Piano Concerto* for one, a lovely piece that Alfred Brendel performs with particular distinction. Berg's *Lulu*, one of the greatest operas of the century. Almost any piece by Webern. And that's just the first group of serialists, known collectively as the Second Viennese School. (As opposed to the First Viennese School, a term nobody uses, which was all the great composers who lived in Vienna—Mozart, Haydn, Beethoven, Schubert, the list goes on—during the late eighteenth and early nineteenth centuries.)

Anyway, you might also try George Rochberg's exquisite *Serenata d'estate*, a lovely summer serenade with a sly quote from Puccini's *Tosca* near the end. Notice I said quote, not theft. And I'm not sure if it's accidental, on purpose, or accidentally on purpose.

If you're feeling a little friskier, you might also want to sample Pierre Boulez's *Le Marteau sans Maître* (The Hammer Without a Master), a delicate song cycle for female voice and small ensemble based on poetry by René Char. And if you really want to get down and funky, check out Bernd Alois Zimmerman's woolly mammoth of an opera, *Die Soldaten* (The Soldiers), which is the very last word on the subject. It's not a bad list, but contains nowhere near the number of pieces one would expect from such a major intellectual movement, one that dominated the two decades following the end of World War II and has yet to be rooted out of academe. Of course, there's always Elliott Carter. . . .

But you don't want to talk about Elliott Carter. You still want to talk about Beethoven. That's why we've spent all this time talking fundamentals. Believe it or not, twelve-tone theory is as fundamental as it comes. Once you understand its basics, the rest of musical theory will seem easy. Now you know why composers have gone to such bother about keys and tonal relationships. The question now is how does knowing any of this—keys, intervals, tones, music history—help you to listen to, say, the *Ninth Symphony*.

It helps in this way: it helps you to avoid what I call the Historic Fallacy.

That's the tendency of many people involved in music to look at history in reverse, as if it were one vast planned and programmed entity, with each composer merely a link in the chain—the teleological approach, as we discussed earlier—instead of as the sum total of a lot of individual choices and accomplishments, haphazard as they may have been.

Let me give you an example. Let's take Scott Joplin. From our vantage point in the late twentieth century, we look back to turn-of-the-century St. Louis and New York City and see a glorified whorehouse pianist, a naif whose ragtime music eventually led to the songs of Irving Berlin and, perhaps, to Jerome Kern's *Show Boat.* We see Joplin's opera, *Treemonisha,* as the aberration in this picture, the fevered delusion of grandeur in a syphilitic brain.

You may object that Joplin is highly regarded today. Didn't Marvin Hamlisch win an Oscar for *The Sting?* Didn't everybody love Joshua Rifkin's recordings of the Joplin rags for Nonesuch? For a while, there, you thought if you heard *The Entertainer* one more time you were going to scream. And you're right: Joplin was popular during the seventies, but for the wrong reasons—not the least of which was his race. You see, the key to Joplin's triumph is not that he was black, but that he was American, and a midwesterner, at that.

But what if we look at Joplin another way, from the front this time, and appreciate him not for what later musicians may or may not have done with his music, but for what he did with it? Then his accomplishment becomes all the more remarkable. His delicate, poetic rags—"Do not play this piece fast. It is never right to play Ragtime fast," the composer often exhorted at the beginning of a piece—have been compared to Brahms waltzes, Chopin mazurkas, or Mozart minuets, but the real comparison, it seems to me, is with Schubert.

Listen, for example, to the gentle 1902 rag, *A Breeze from Alabama.* This is not one of the better known rags, like the *Maple Leaf* or the *Pineapple,* but its very unfamiliarity throws Joplin's gifts into high relief. Listen, especially, to the second theme in F major and tell me that the ghost of Schubert (who died of the same disease that killed Joplin) isn't looking over his shoulder, smiling. In their grace and bounce, Joplin rags remind me more of Schubert dances than anything else.

Now, how did Schubert wander all the way from Vienna to Texarkana, Texas, and Sedalia, Missouri? With all the fuss over Joplin around the time of *The Sting* and the premiere of *Treemonisha* in Houston, everyone was much too concerned with *whom* Joplin influenced than to address the more interesting question, *by whom?* Overlooked is the role a German-born music teacher in

Texarkana played in young Scott's early musical education. This man, unnamed by Joplin but tentatively identified by an enterprising musicologist a few years ago as a man named Weiss, was probably a Jewish German emigré who played the classics, and spoke to Scott of the great composers and the famous operas.

Those days with Weiss seem to have been the extent of Joplin's formal musical education, but their impact on him was tremendous. When you listen to the Joplin rags today, try to think of them not as red-light district sing-alongs but as tiny, formal gems of melody and harmony. The stride bass—the oom-pah left hand—is just a structural device, like the Alberti bass of the early classical period (that's the broken chord, a la Phil Glass, that makes up the left hand parts in eighteenth century sonatas and sonatinas. Mozart's famous C major sonata, which every beginning pianist has a go at, has an Alberti bass). Joplin's triumph was to weld the instruction he got from Weiss to the form of ragtime and to create some of the most perfect piano miniatures ever written by an American. *That's* why he's great, not because Irving Berlin piggybacked a third-rate song onto what was already then a dying art form.

Alas, poor Joplin did not have the advantages that Will Marion Cook—a tremendously underappreciated black American composer from about the same time—did. Cook, a fine violinist, was educated at Oberlin, in Berlin, and at the National Conservatory of Music in New York, where he studied under Dvorak. He wrote the music to the show that is credited as being the first all-black musical to succeed on Broadway: *Clorindy, the Origin of the Cakewalk*. The only surviving number from this 1898 show has been recorded on New World Records; it is the overture, *Darktown Is Out Tonight*. Check it out.

So let's summarize. We've talked about a lot of things in this chapter, but can we boil it all down to a few words you can take with you into the concert hall?

Here goes: by understanding the circumstances under which a composer wrote, we gain a better appreciation of his work than by looking back with 20-20 hindsight and congratulating him for what others learned from him. Bach didn't codify Baroque practice by reading a theory book; Schoenberg didn't follow a tone row chart while inventing the twelve-tone system; and Joplin didn't give a hoot about Irving Berlin.

Let me give you a good example of the Historic Fallacy, ripped right from the pages of the New York *Times*, whose staff is consistently among the worst offenders. In his review of Rossini's grand opera *William Tell* at la Scala in late 1988, one of the *Times* critics, after proclaiming the rather obscure opera's historical importance, lambasted the piece for not being the equal of later works by other composers: "Only think of the speech in *Norma* [by Bellini] restraining the Druids, Elena's incitement of the oppressed Sicilians in [Verdi's] *Vespri Siciliani*, Amonasro's defense of patriotism in defeat in *Aida* [Verdi again]. *William Tell* needs something to set beside these."

Well, excuuuuuuse me! The critic goes on, waxing rhetorical as he further pummels his straw man:

"Is it fair to make comparisons with the mature Verdi, who had forged a harmonic-dramatic language unavailable to Rossini? One could look in other directions and speak of [Beethoven's] *Fidelio* or of Mozart's operas"—the proper comparison, as we know—"but it is Verdi's presence one feels while seeing *William Tell*, and perhaps that says something else. The kind of opera that Schiller's themes suggest, the vision of opera toward which *Tell* inclines at moments, *demanded that a Verdi come into being*." (Emphasis mine.) You can't get a much clearer, or sillier, articulation of the Historic Fallacy than that. And this from a critic who considers himself a scholar.

Let's look at the facts. Rossini wrote *William Tell*, his last major work, in 1829. After that, at the age of thirty-seven, he abruptly retired from opera composing, lived to grow fat and happy, and died in 1868, honored and beloved. Bellini's *Norma* came along two years after *Tell*, while the two Verdi operas alluded to are from 1855 and 1871. To use Amonasro's aria from *Aida*—one of the relatively better pieces in an output that also includes a long string of disasters and failures—as a stick with which to beat poor

Rossini is a little like complaining that a car from 1946 is not as technologically advanced as one from 1988. But it's typical of this school of "thought."

Okay, you'll probably never see *William Tell* in your life. Besides, you already know the Overture—the Lone Ranger, right? You just want me to tell you how to sit still through the *Ninth*.

Now we've come to it, then. The simple, one-word answer is: patience. The simple, two-word answer is: patience and knowledge. The simple three-word answer is: patience, knowledge, and imagination. Other than that, you're on your own.

Armed with what you've learned here, and what you'll surely want to discover on your own, you can now approach the most fearsome pieces of music secure in the knowledge that you've got their number. You know how to think of Beethoven: not as an early, imperfect version of Bruckner or Mahler or Wagner, but as the man who explored and exploded the boundaries of the classical symphony; that's the knowledge part. Then, using your imagination, put yourself in the place of someone who lived in the 1820s and listening to this revolutionary music for the first time. Imagine the excitement, the thrill of hearing a human voice for the first time in a symphony. Picture the shudder that ran down everyone's spine when they first heard the tremendous clashing dissonance that opens the finale.

Above all, remember that Beethoven has a lot to say and you must allow him the time to say it. No ten-minute attention spans need apply in the concert hall; there are no commercial breaks, no words from our sponsor. Listen for Beethoven's themes—the melodies, if you will—and follow how he changes and develops them. Listen to the way he orchestrates his music, that is, how he gives this theme to the flute and that one to the violins and this one to the trumpets. (Beethoven's orchestration is not very good; it just proves that even a genius has his weak points.) Listen to the power and the urgency of his utterances and let these qualities wash over you. If you have any soul at all, it will soon be harkening to the message. In the end, there is just you, the night, and the music.

Surrender to it. That is the road to mastery. That is the zen of music, the high like no other.

How do you listen? With your ears, your heart, and your soul.

INTERLUDE: SCHUMANN AND BRAHMS

What is it about central Europe that has produced so many great composers? From the time of Bach on, the great German and Germanic composers have come in waves, surging across the Continent, lapping at the shores of Great Britain, and penetrating deep into Russia. This is not to downgrade the substantial accomplishment of the Italians—who, after all, taught the Germans how to write music during the early Baroque era—or the French who, from the time of Lully on, have created a distinctive musical style that mirrors the savoir-faire of their culture in general. Or the British, who boasted a line of outstanding composers during the Renaissance—Weelkes, Wilbye, Tallis, Dowland—that culminated in the achievement of Purcell, then took a two hundred year vacation until Sir Edward Elgar emerged in the late nineteenth century. Or the Russians, who since Glinka have forged and maintained their own highly characteristic musical language.

Still, when we talk about the great composers, we tend to mean the great German and Austrian composers. They are the bedrock of our concert programming; any discussion of classical music must necessarily begin with them. The two men we are considering—Robert Schumann and Johannes Brahms—span the nineteenth century, the heart of the repertory. Yet their lives were also intertwined in more personal, significant ways: as critic and discovery; as mentor and pupil; as lover of the same woman. Even more than Liszt's or Chopin's, the story of Schumann and Brahms—and Clara—is the story of romanticism.

Robert Schumann was born in Zwickau, near Leipzig; like Wagner, he was from Saxony, a flat, agricultural province of Germany that also gave the world the British royal family (which diplomatically changed its name to the House of Windsor from the more ethnic *Saxe, Coburg und Gotha* during World War I; Prince Albert, Queen Victoria's husband, spoke German and wrote *lieder* a la Schubert).

From childhood, Schumann was cursed with a neurasthenic nature. Madness ran in the family, and Schumann was convinced that someday it would claim him, too. (That it eventually did must have been small consolation.) His father August, a bookseller, suffered from a nervous disorder; his sister, Emilia, killed herself. Young Robert immersed himself in the romantic novels of Jean Paul and Novalis, E. T. A. Hoffmann and Brentano, and would soon enough be recreating their hothouse atmosphere in his music.

Despite her son's literary predilections, Schumann's mother pushed him into the law. He went to Leipzig, where he wound up going to concerts, practicing the piano, chasing girls, and smoking cigars all day, instead of attending to his studies; even a year in Heidelberg failed to produce much in the way of legal eagling, although it was apparently there that he contracted the syphilis that eventually drove him mad and killed him.

Back in Leipzig in 1830, he met the woman who would change his life. Actually, she was a girl, the eleven-year-old daughter of his piano teacher, Friedrich Wieck. Clara was not only a brilliant prodigy, but her father's great love and his fierce protectiveness would eventually make both her and Robert's life miserable. But that was in the future.

Schumann moved in with the Wiecks, Friedrich's vow to make him a great pianist within three years ringing in his ears. He practiced furiously, dedicated and impatient. Too impatient, as it turned out: in an effort to strengthen his fourth finger, he invented a harness that immobilized it while he played. This of course had the opposite effect, and ruined him for life. Now there was nothing for him but to become a composer. It was a calling he was ready for. "On sleepless nights," he wrote, "I am conscious of a mission which rises before me like a distant peak."

And Clara was just the person to help him accomplish that mission. Thrown together, they fell in love. Schumann tried to show old Wieck that he was responsible: he began writing music criticism (he discovered Chopin with the famous notice, "Hats off, gentleman! A genius!") and even founded his own magazine, the *Neue Zeitschrift für Musik*. But Wieck would have none of it. His only daughter, marrying a crippled journalist who wanted to be a composer? Surely she could do better than Schumann.

It got ugly. Wieck embarked on a planned campaign of character assassination, imputing to Schumann alcoholism and unreliability, among other things. The lovers finally had to go to court and, after three years of wrangling (finally, some good use for Schumann's education), they were married without Wieck's consent in 1840. Clara was twenty-one.

Clara was everything to Robert. Their relationship called forth his most glorious music. (She, in turn, bore him eight children, five of whom lived.) First came the piano music, including the two sonatas (1835 and 1838), the masterpiece of *Carnaval* (1835), the tender *Kinderszenen* of 1837, and the magnificent *Fantasie in C major* of 1838. Then, the year they were married, came the songs—150 of them in a single year—including the *Frauenliebe und -leben* and the *Dichterliebe*. Practically at a single stroke, Schumann had won a place for himself not only among the greatest composers for the piano but the greatest song writers as well.

At Clara's urging, Schumann turned next to orchestral music, and between 1841 and 1850 wrote all four of his symphonies, as well as the dashing *Piano Concerto in A minor*. Then, less happily, came the opera *Genoveva* and the incidental music to the drama, *Manfred*. Schumann's gift was for the smaller forms. But his health was deteriorating rapidly, and he had to give up his post as music director in Düsseldorf. In 1854, he began to suffer severe hallucinations; the note "A" was ringing in his ears; the ghosts of Schubert and Mendelssohn brought him music from the next world; wild animals were trying to devour him. In desperation, he leaped into the Rhine.

Although he lived another two years, that was the end for poor Schumann. He was committed to an asylum, where he died on July 29, 1856, attended to the last by his beloved Clara. And by a young man from Hamburg named Johannes Brahms.

Brahms was one of Schumann's discoveries. In one of his last articles, he hailed the young Brahms as the savior of German music. (Schumann's critical prescience was remarkable. He spotted Chopin on the basis of the early, and unrepresentative, *La ci darem Variations* for piano and orchestra; of Brahms, he knew the early piano sonatas.) Brahms was the young eagle to come out of the north to rescue German music from the depredations of Liszt and Wagner and the rest of the Music of the Future gang.

It was a wise choice. Brahms had grown up on the tough docksides of Hamburg, playing the piano in the city's notorious bordellos as a child to help his penurious father make ends meet. The experience ruined Brahms as far as women were concerned; he never married and his sex life was conducted among prostitutes. "That was my first impression of women," he told a friend years later. "And you expect me to honor them as you do?"

The handsome, slender, fair-haired boy met Schumann in 1853, introduced by the violinist Joseph Joachim. "Brahms to see me," noted Schumann in his diary, "(a genius)." As Wieck had done for him, Schumann insisted that Brahms move into his house, and Brahms was there, a sturdy shoulder for Clara, during the last three years of Robert's tragic life. And while Clara wore the widow's weeds for the rest of her days (she also stopped composing), Brahms fell violently, passionately, hopelessly in love with her. He stayed that way forever.

After Schumann's death, a change came over Brahms. The slender youth disappeared, replaced seemingly overnight by the gruff, bearded Beethoven manqué. In 1862, Brahms moved to Vienna, where he stayed until his death, and he stalked the streets of Beethoven's city in much the same way the Bonn master had done a generation before: head down, scarf billowing. His temper was short, his insults quick. No one was safe. Once the composer Max Bruch brought Brahms the score of a new oratorio and asked him what he thought of it. A few days later, while sitting in a café, Brahms and Bruch heard an organ grinder playing. "Listen, Bruch," exclaimed Brahms. "That fellow has gotten hold of your

Arminius!" His was not the kind of personality to win friends and influence people.

Not that he cared. Brahms's world was music, and a very good judge of it he was too. Brahms was a great score collector, and had bagged Mozart's autograph score of the *Symphony No. 40 in G minor* as a prize trophy, along with Wagner's *Tannhäuser;* although Brahms was Wagner's arch-enemy, at least musically speaking, he didn't let personal feelings interfere with his judgment. (Later, Wagner asked for and got the score back, trading Brahms an autograph of *Das Rheingold* in its place.) Long before it was fashionable, Brahms was also a connoisseur of early music—in those days, this meant Bach.

Brahms was a traditionalist by nature. At a time when Wagner and Liszt were exploding old forms and inventing new ones, Brahms was still (as they saw it) bumping along down the symphony-sonata allegro track. His great works were written in classic forms: four symphonies; two piano concertos, one violin concerto, one concerto for violin and cello; sonatas for various instruments; a *Requiem*; sets of themes and variations. There were no tone poems and no operas.

Still, Brahms infused everything with new life. The *Requiem* was not a Mass, but a setting of German texts, hence its name: *Ein Deutsches Requiem.* It was in memory of his mother. He memorialized Clara, too, in the slow movement of the *Piano Concerto No. 1* and, after her death in 1896, the *Vier Ernste Gesänge.* (He also tipped his hat to Robert in the opening theme of his *Third Symphony,* whose aggressive, driving melody pops up—although lyrically—in several Schumann symphonies. Possibly it had some hidden, special meaning.) The next year he developed cancer of the liver, the same disease that had killed his father. On March 7, 1897, he managed to stagger from his sickbed to the Musikverein to hear Hans Richter conduct the *Symphony No. 4.* The audience, knowing of his illness and sensing this might be the last hurrah, greeted him with a prolonged ovation. Brahms died a month later. He was 63.

If a composer's soul is mirrored in his music, then Brahms has left us a clear self-portrait. Forget the bluff exterior and the shabby clothes; the inner man was taut and logical. Even in the most difficult pieces, there is no show-for-show's-sake in Brahms. His piano music, for example, is notably lacking in the flashy scales that mark Liszt's and Chopin's. Instead, all is big chords and leaping octaves and his characteristic rhythmic device of three beats against two or four. Simple as it looks on the page, though, it brims with hidden details, mostly polyphonic. Brahms had learned much from Bach and the other baroque composers whose music he knew, and the inner voices of Brahms's music are among music's great glories. (Schumann has this element too, although not so pronounced.)

When we think of Brahms, we see him in the famous painting: seated at the piano, his short legs barely reaching the pedals, his hands crossing in a typically Brahmsian bit of keyboard writing, a cigar stuck in his mouth. (Sometimes, as Freud said, a cigar is only a cigar. And sometimes it's not.) Probably he is playing one of the late piano pieces, those remarkable little confessionals that go by the name of *Klavierstücke* (piano pieces), *Fantasies* or *Intermezzi*— the fruits of Op. 116, 117, 118, and 119, ballades, intermezzos, and romances. They speak with all the passion, tenderness, and sorrow that in life he could never utter.

4

OPERA—
IT'S NOT AS BAD
AS IT SOUNDS

I know what you're thinking. We've made it this far, past the Scylla of sonatas and the Charybdis of concertos. Now the most dangerous obstacle of all looms just ahead: opera. How will we ever get past it?

Don't worry. I am about to let you in on classical music's deepest, darkest secret. Just like the lady in Molière who was astonished one day to discover that she had been speaking prose all of her life, so, in one form or another, have you been listening to opera. And you didn't even know it! So why are you afraid of it now?

Well, let us count the ways: spinto, fach, heldentenor, chest voice, recitative, da capo arias, Bayreuth, even the word opera itself . . . the list goes on. And we haven't even mentioned any composers or works yet. Opera, it seems, bristles with arcane terminology, brandished and bandied about with reckless abandon by the cognoscenti during intermissions at the Met. Names of long dead singers like Caruso, Melba, and Calvé (the rule is: last names only when the person is retired or dead, first names only if he or she is still alive, e.g., [Franco] Corelli and [Leonard] Warren but Placido [Domingo] and Luciano [Pavarotti]) are invoked as if the speaker were expecting the dearly departed to walk on stage at any moment. Arias are referred to en passant in their French, Italian, or German titles—"Mon coeur s'ouvre a ta voix," "Nessun dorma," "Martern aller artern"—or by a mysterious phrase like the "Prize Song." It's enough to make you wonder when the next swan boat leaves.

Fortunately, it's not at all as intimidating as it appears. (As Mark

Twain once said, "Wagner's music is not as bad as it sounds." And he was right.) For one thing, operaphiles have had years to add to their storehouses of knowledge, and over time have developed a kind of shorthand (or shorttalk) when discussing their favorite art form. If you are going to talk baseball with a Red Sox fan, are you going to bother to explain what you mean by, say, "Game Six" or "Bucky Dent" or "Bill Buckner"? Of course not. So don't expect the opera world to bend over backward to help you, either. It's a tough, dog-eat-dog world out there; during the intervals (as the British call intermissions), one-upmanship is everything.

But even if you think that *Andrea Chenier* used to be a power forward for the Knicks and that *Rigoletto* is a trattoria in Little Italy, you are not totally ignorant. Before there were symphony orchestras and public instrumental recitals, there was opera. For what is opera but a sung play, an entertainment with music? So what if you've never sat through the 19 hours of Wagner's *Ring* cycle? If you have ever heard *West Side Story* or *Les Misérables* or even *Tommy*, you've heard an opera. I'll prove it in a minute. But first a little history.

This may come as a shock, but opera is meant to be *enjoyable*. At least, that was the thinking of the nobles in Renaissance Florence, at whose courts opera was invented. Only they didn't call it "opera," they called it "melodramma" or "dramma per musica." (The word *opera* in Italian is the plural of *opus* and means simply "works.") Whatever you call it, this novel admixture of music, song, poetry, dance, and drama was meant to hark back to the ancient Greek theatrical tradition. Obviously, such an activity was highly speculative, and composers like Claudio Monteverdi (composer of the earliest opera still in the repertoire, *The Coronation of Poppea*) imbued it with fresh new life. Although opera began as a royal entertainment, it quickly spread to the general public; by 1637, Venice had its first opera house and, soon enough, there were ten.

Opera spread quickly, across the Alps and into northern Europe, where, aside from England, it took firm root. The principal English operatic composer, Henry Purcell, died at the age of 36 in

1695; 15 years later, the carpetbagging George Frideric Handel arrived from Germany with his box-office brand of Italian opera and set back the cause of native composition in the sceptered isle by a century. Still, opera developed internationally so quickly that by 1762 it already had need for its first great reformer, Christoph Willibald Gluck, whose *Orfeo ed Euridice* of that year purged the genre of much of its rodomontade and paved the way for the greater genius of Mozart a few years later.

"When I undertook to write music for *Alceste*," Gluck wrote in 1767 of his next great work, "I resolved to divest it entirely of all those abuses, introduced into it either by the mistaken vanity of singers or by the too great complaisance of composers, which have so long disfigured Italian opera and made of the most splendid and most beautiful of spectacles the most ridiculous and wearisome."

What was Gluck referring to? Exactly those things that you find so risible. Opera, Gluck felt, should be strong, simple, and clear. It should not be obscure, florid, or silly. It should act directly on the emotions of the listeners. It should not be devoted to meaningless vocal display. Opera, in other words, should be about drama, not about singing. It is a lesson we have to learn every century or so.

The concept of music that underpins a drama, that gives it breadth, depth, scope and, finally, life, has a long and ancient history. We tend to think of its manifestation exclusively as opera, but it goes by many names: *Singspiel* (the German form, with spoken dialogue and musical interludes; Mozart's *The Magic Flute* is a good example), which leads directly to the *Broadway Musical Comedy*, whose ancestry also includes the *Viennese Operetta*. With the invention of film, this art form leaped from the proscenium stage to the wide screen; in many respects, the greatest American operas of the early twentieth century were silent movies, just as, in mid-century, they were Broadway shows. Today, oddly enough, the greatest American operas are exactly that—operas.

The principle behind opera is that the music should give life to the characters on stage, to flesh them out, to make them breathe. Music—not the libretto (the lyrics) or the story (in a Broadway show, that would be called the "book"; in opera, it's also the libretto)—is opera's lifeblood. Who among us reads opera librettos for poetry, despite the great works of Lorenzo da Ponte (Mozart's librettist)? Who goes to the opera to hum the scenery, the opera-director-as-superstar era we currently inhabit, to the contrary notwithstanding? When opera is reduced to its irreducible element, what do you have? That's right, the music.

Okay, okay, I can hear you saying, I think I'm beginning to catch on. Maybe opera isn't as arcane as I used to think. But what does this all mean in practical terms?

I'm glad you asked. (Now we get to the fun part.)

The opera may not be over until the fat lady sings, but it's not basically about fat ladies. Granted, opera stages are populated with great singing Hefty bags and man-mountains who shake the earth with their cries and rattle the fundaments of their fans in the audience. But what are they crying about? Sex, that's what. Or thinking about having sex. Or wanting to have sex. Or preventing someone else from having sex. Whether the performers are fat is irrelevant: opera is not about fat people at all! It's not even about singing! It's about sex!

This is opera's dirty little secret, so well hidden that for years healthy, normal, well-adjusted American men and women have abandoned its manifest pleasures to the canary fanciers whose intermission conversations are devoted to arguing the relative merits of singers. Such chatter probably has served to drive away more potential patrons than Florence Foster Jenkins in tinsel and tulle as the Angel of Inspiration, unsteadily essaying the high F as Mozart's Queen of the Night.

(The ineffable FFJ—"FloFo," she might be called in modern parlance—was the world's worst, albeit best intentioned, soprano, whose greatest triumph came on October 25, 1944 when she rented Carnegie Hall for an unforgettable evening of song, accompanied by pianist Cosme McMoon. She was seventy-six years old at the time, and died a month later.)

Don't believe me? Well, check it out:

A BAKER'S DOZEN OF FAMOUS OPERA PLOTS

Mozart: *The Marriage of Figaro.* Horny count wants to sleep with saucy serving wench on the night she marries his valet. Horny pageboy wants to sleep with countess while count is otherwise engaged. (To make things a little more piquant, the pageboy is played by a soprano. Opera is loaded with transvestism like this.) All hell breaks loose, but it all ends well. Hit song: Figaro's aria "Non più andrai" ("You're in the army now, you little rascal"), quoted by Mozart himself in *Don Giovanni.*

Così fan tutte. Two soldiers swear their girlfriends (who are sisters) will always be faithful. Old roué Don Alfonso bets them they won't be. Boys spend rest of opera trying to seduce each other's girl. Guess who wins the bet? Hit song: the duet for the two sisters, "Ah guarda, sorella." ("Sister, watch out!")

Don Giovanni. Spanish rake sneaks in titled ladies' windows—object: intimacy—while sturdy servant Leporello keeps track of his master's conquests—object, bragging (1,003 in Spain alone). Oops! The don kills Donna Anna's dad in a duel, and when Giovanni later invites the old man's stone monument to dinner, there's the devil to pay. Hit song: Leporello's "catalog aria," "Madamina! il catalogo." ("Madam! Take a look at this little black book!")

Bizet: *Carmen.* The world's most popular opera, even if it is mighty long. Hotheaded country bumpkin soldier Don José gets hots for trampy Gypsy cigarette girl in old Seville, is cashiered from army and falls in with smugglers. When flashy toreador rival steals his girl, there's nothing left for Don José but murder most foul. Hit song: a tough choice, since just about every tune is a winner. But probably the *Toreador Song,* by a bull's whiskers.

Verdi: *Rigoletto.* Lecherous duke makes seducing women his life's work, and lets the chips fall where they may. Alas, virginal daughter of his court jester gets bagged and tagged when typically operatic case of mistaken identity strikes. Hit song: "La donna é mobile" ("Women are fickle").

***La Traviata* (The Fallen Woman).** High-class Parisian hooker falls for innocent young country lad, then nobly spurns him when his insufferably meddlesome dad pleads family honor. Of course, she dies horribly of consumption. Hit song: "Sempre libera" ("Always Free," or "I Gotta Be Me").

La Forza del destino **(The Force of Destiny).** The Force of Coincidence, is more like it. Leonora's sexual hysteria turns into religious fervor when her father is accidentally killed by her lover, Don Alvaro, who is part Inca Indian. She becomes a nun and goes to live in a cave; meanwhile, her brother Don Carlo—not to be confused with the Don Carlos who is the hero of a later Verdi opera, just as this Leonora is not to be confused with an earlier Verdi heroine in the highly risible *Il Trovatore*—won't rest until he gets revenge. Of course, it ends badly for everybody. Hit tune: none, unless you count the various curses, oaths, and pleas for forgiveness the various characters utter incessantly.

Aida. The world's second most popular opera, even if it is mighty, mighty long. In ancient Egypt, stud war hero Radames secretly loves swarthy slave girl Aida who, unknown to everybody, is daughter of the bad-ass Ethiopian chieftain who is the pharoah's mortal enemy. When the bitchy princess Amneris gets wind of the affair, it's curtains for Radames, who gets buried alive. To make things nicer, Aida joins him and they suffocate together while singing a duet. Hit tune: "Celeste Aida" (Heavenly Aida). Favorite sport: listening to the tenor strangle on the final, supposedly quiet, high B-flat.

Wagner: *The Ring of the Nibelung.* Nineteen hours of fun, a long time ago in a land far away. In first scene, horny dwarf gets teased by topless mermaids, goes wild and steals their chunk of gold from the middle of the Rhine river. Gods, giants, more dwarfs, and even a few humans chase the gold up hill and down dale for the next three days. Brother sleeps with sister in most famous instance of operatic incest; priapic father/god Wotan sleeps with (a) unidentified human woman, (b) earth mother goddess, (c) possibly, own wife (not shown). Giant gets lovesick over goddess; hero goes gaga over Valkyrie; everyone comes to grief at the end as world is destroyed by fire and water. Hit song: "The Ride of the Valkyries" in the second opera in the cycle, *Die Walküre. Ho-jo-to-ho* and have a nice day!

Tristan und Isolde. Hot-blooded Irish princess meets passionate knight from Brittany, wants to kill him, then (after downing love potion) wants to sleep with him. Unfortunately, she's married to his uncle, a humorless old bore from Cornwall. All-Celtic family squabble ends like *Hamlet*, with nearly everybody dead. Hit tune: Isolde's "Liebestod," or Love-Death. Bonus: most famous example of coitus interruptus in musical history (Act Two). She *has* to be Irish.

Puccini: *Tosca.* Fiery diva has mad romance with Italian painter/patriot, but falls under the lustful gaze of gross chief of secret police in Rome. Shameless tease pretends to respond, then stabs him to death in his bedroom. Too late! Boyfriend gets stood up against a wall and shot, so Tosca takes a header off the Castel Sant'Angelo and into the Tiber (or, more likely, onto the road). A "shabby little shocker," as Joe Kerman once remarked, but nobody seems to mind. Hit tune: "Vissi d'arte" ("I Live for Art and Love").

Madama Butterfly. The world's third most popular opera, even if it is stupefyingly boring. Heartless bastard Lieutenant Pinkerton pulls into old Nagasaki and marries cute little bit of local fluff named Cio-cio San, then sails away again, leaving her with child. Butterfly expects him back any day until Mrs. Kate Pinkerton shows up to tell her the truth: ain't gonna be no Lieutenant Pinkerton 'round here anymore. What next? Why, suicide, of course. Hit tune: "Un bel di" (One fine day).

Richard Strauss: *Elektra.* Fiery Greek girl plots vengeance after dear old dad Agamemnon is axe-murdered in the bathtub by slut-bitch mom Klytemnestra and wimpy lover Aegisthus. When long-lost brother Orestes returns home, the House of Atreus has a fine old family reunion. Elektra gets so excited she dances herself to death. (Do I hear a waltz? I do indeed.) Note: this Strauss is Richard, and not either Johann, Sr. or Jr. Be prepared.

My summations are a little irreverent, of course, but you get the idea: opera has always been intended as an extraordinarily communicative art form. Because opera is so expressive—because it has so many theatrical elements that go into its makeup—composers have always been drawn to big, powerful subjects for operatic treatment. There are, of course, many wonderful comic operas. The three operas Mozart wrote with da Ponte are all comedies, including *Don Giovanni*, which has considerable comedic elements. Wagner wrote *Die Meistersinger von Nürnberg* (The Mastersingers of Nuremberg)—not exactly a laugh riot, to be sure, but light by Wagnerian standards. Verdi, at the end of his life, wrote *Falstaff*, Strauss composed *Der Rosenkavalier* (The Knight of the Silver Rose), and Puccini wrote *Gianni Schicchi* as part of a three-opera evening called *Il Trittico*. But there can be no doubt that the best operatic themes are still blood, guts, and sex.

In the twentieth century, composers have adhered to the norm. Think of the great modern operas (and, contrary to firmly held opinion, there *are* great modern operas). Alban Berg's *Wozzeck*—one of the two or three greatest operas ever written—is about a miserable soldier who murders his mistress and then drowns himself, while the same composer's *Lulu* unblinkingly chronicles the career of a downwardly mobile, tawdry temptress who ruins the lives of nearly everyone she touches, descends the social ladder from high-class tart and kept woman to common street whore, and is finally murdered by Jack the Ripper in a London hovel. Cheerful stuff!

Dmitri Shostakovich's *Lady Macbeth of Mtzensk* is a shocking tale of adultery and murder in old Russia; the rape scene, with its suggestive trombone slides, is one of the most vivid depictions of sexual intercourse in music (rivaling the all-time champ, the whooping horns in the overture to Richard Strauss's *Der Rosenkavalier*). *Lady Macbeth* gave Stalin the willies and for years, this work was performed only in its bowdlerized version as *Katerina Ismailova*. (Shostakovich's first, and only other, opera is *The Nose*, a grotesque comedy about an ambulatory schnoz based on the story by Gogol.)

Benjamin Britten's *Peter Grimes* concerns a funny old fisherman who may or may not be a child abuser, while the same composer's *Death in Venice* is about an aging German writer who falls in love with a young Polish boy and, smitten, stays on to die of cholera when an epidemic sweeps the Adriatic coast. Britten's own homosexuality gives the latter a certain, shall we say, authenticity of feeling.

I would be remiss if I didn't mention a special passion of mine, the music theater works of Carl Orff, the German composer best known for his lusty choral work, *Carmina Burana.* It is fashionable—at least, it used to be—to dismiss Orff as a simple-minded reactionary against the complexity of twentieth century music, but there is nothing elementary about such works as the charming Bavarian fable, *Der Mond* (The Moon), or the hair-raising Greek tragedy, *Oedipus der Tyrann.* In *Carmina Burana,* Orff stripped his music down to fundamentals, melody and rhythm, and never looked back; each succeeding work, it seemed, was sparer than the last. His Greek operas (he also wrote *Antigonae,* among other pieces) were an attempt to reinterpret the original spirit of the Greek theater—there really is nothing new under the sun—and while they are perhaps best appreciated by German-speaking audiences (the texts are Hölderlin's translations of Sophocles), they deserve a wider hearing.

One departure from all this gloom and doom has been the operas of Philip Glass, the Baltimore-born composer whose name has become synonymous with a musical style known as minimalism (see separate essay on the minimalists), and who, in many ways, is Orff's spiritual godson. Glass's first opera, *Einstein on the Beach,* was only vaguely about Einstein—indeed, it was only vaguely about plot at all. But his more conventional second and third operas, *Satyagraha* and *Akhnaten,* have stronger narrative structures. Not too conventional, though: *Satyagraha,* perhaps the best opera of the latter twentieth century, the story of Mohandas Gandhi's early years in South Africa (where he developed his revolutionary philosophy of non-violent resistance to authority) is told through the action on stage, not the words. *Akhnaten,* meanwhile, explores the short, unhappy life of the pharoah who may have been history's first monotheist.

Not sure-fire subjects. But Glass, even at the risk of sometimes repeating himself, has steadfastly gone his own way. He has set texts as disparate as Poe's *The Fall of the House of Usher*, Doris Lessing's *The Making of the Representative for Planet Eight*, and the Chinese-American playwright David Henry Hwang's fantasy, *1,000 Airplanes on the Roof*. At a time when many were saying opera was dead, the former taxi driver and steel foundry worker Glass came along to prove the fat lady had not sung yet.

One other minimalist work deserves mention here: John Adams's *Nixon in China*, first performed in Houston in October 1987. With a text by Alice Goodman, and as staged by Peter Sellars, *Nixon* sharply divided critics at its opening. Those who disliked it couldn't have been more wrong. *Nixon* is one of the most accomplished first operas in history, surely calculated, stunningly realized, and fully equal artistically to the extravagant demands of its subject, President Nixon's epochal 1972 powwow with Mao in the Forbidden City. From the spooky, haunted opening through the devastating interview with Mao (the wailing saxophone is reminiscent of Berg's use of the instrument in *Lulu*) to the magnificent banquet that is its final scene, the first act of *Nixon* is a brilliantly calculated theatrical entertainment. The second act, which turns into a hallucination for the Nixons while at a ballet, is a little more problematic, but the third act, a long meditation by the principals on their lives, each wrapped in his or her own solitary thoughts, brings the piece to a daring, effective close. American opera has never been healthier.

A word about so-called "rock opera," a short-lived genre that flourished briefly in the late sixties and early seventies. There weren't many of them: *Tommy* and *Quadrophenia* by The Who; The Kinks' single-album, *Lola vs. Powerman and the Underground* and *Arthur*; Tim Rice and Andrew Lloyd Webber's *Jesus Christ Superstar*. That's about it, although the label hung on for a while, draped around the neck of such clearly non-rock operas as the Rice-Lloyd Webber *Evita*. The Beatles, of course, began the whole notion of concept albums with 1967's *Sgt. Pepper's Lonely Hearts Club Band* (imitated by the Rolling Stones with *Their Satanic Majesties Request*) and then polished it to a fare-thee-well with the greatest (and, alas, unstageable) rock opera ever, their swan song, *Abbey Road*. If there is a better extended piece of rock music than Side Two of *Abbey Road*, I don't know what it is.

The very existence of rock opera, however, proves my point that opera admits of much wider definition than most people think. Even if the impulse came to naught in the mid-seventies—as Iron Butterfly and Led Zeppelin degenerated into Motley Crüe and T Rex—it reflected the feeling at the time that art was possible, even in as commercial medium as rock. Remember Ars Nova, which tried to wed rock to classical tunes? The Incredible String Band, born at least a decade too early to cash in on both New Age and the Celtic revival? The Soft Machine? The good that these groups did lived on after them, and eventually pointed the way for Tangerine Dream, the Talking Heads, and Phil Glass to peacefully coexist on the fringes of the rock-classical avant-garde.

Even if you never cared for rock, though, you got exposure to the operatic principle from another medium: the movies. At the dawn of movie history, there was music; indeed, music, not words, was once the real dramatic voice of films. In the silent era, French composer Camille Saint-Saens wrote the score for *L'Assassinat du Duc de Buise*, and D. W. Griffith's classic, *Broken Blossoms*, was outfitted with music by the Louisiana-born nineteenth century composer and pianist, Louis Moreau Gottschalk. The *Nibelungenlied* films of the great German director Fritz Lang were retrofitted with tunes from Wagner's *Ring* cycle, although Lang preferred the original scores by Gottfried Huppertz as being more attuned to the expressionistic spirit of his movies. The early Edison kinescope of *Frankenstein* was released with a cue sheet that called for music from Carl Maria von Weber's opera *Der Freischütz* to herald the monster, and the song *Annie Laurie* for the domestic scenes.

From the beginning, the technique of silent film scoring was based on the Wagnerian principle of leitmotifs, those recurring little tunes—Debussy derided them as "calling cards"—that signify persons, places, things, and emotions. The idea was not original with Wagner, although he perfected it. (In the *Ring*, for example, the tempest that opens the second opera, *Die Walküre*, is a first cousin to the storm of Beethoven's *Pastoral Symphony*.) But it caught on big and even while rejecting Wagnerism in his own operatic masterpiece, *Pelleas et Melisande*, Debussy made use of the technique. Soon, everybody was doin' it: in a 1921 review of Robert Wiene's horror masterpiece, *The Cabinet of Dr. Caligari*, the American composer Bernard Rogers, writing in the magazine *Musical America*, noted that "the score is built up on the leitmotif system; quite in the Wagnerian manner."

Explicitly in the Wagnerian manner was Hans Erdmann's music for *Nosferatu*, F. W. Murnau's great cinematic treatment of the *Dracula* story. (Erdmann also scored Lang's *Das Testament des Dr. Mabuse* and wrote a handbook on film scoring, published in 1927. He died in 1948.) Murnau's film was subtitled *Eine Symphonie des Grauens* (A Symphony of Horror), and was meant to be seen in conjunction with an appropriately spooky score. Erdmann and Murnau worked closely together, matching sound to image. Erdmann's *Fantastisch-romantische Suite* is all ominous kettle drums for Count Orlok, all sweetness and light for the heroine, Ellen, who weeps when a flower is picked. The only outright borrowing in it comes near the end, when Max Schreck (great pseudonym! "Schreck" means "horror" in German. Great teeth, too!) tarries a little too long at the delectable Ellen's neckside; the sliding key changes of the middle section of Chopin's Op. 15, No: 3 *G-minor Nocturne* signal the end of his reign of terror as the sun comes up and melts him away.

The great days of the German cinema, though, died with the Weimar Republic. The action moved west, to Hollywood, where both native-born and expatriate composers churned out score after lavish score in the service of Tinseltown. From Vienna came the erstwhile operatic wunderkind Erich Wolfgang Korngold—"there's more corn than gold" in his scores, one wag cracked—who made the transition smoothly from the opera *Die Tote Stadt* to the film *The Private Lives of Elizabeth and Essex*, among many others. Korngold liked his movie music so much that he later turned some of his themes into a *Symphony in F-sharp*.

Bernard Herrmann went in the other direction, first achieving prominence as the composer of Orson Welles's *Citizen Kane* and, best of all, Alfred Hitchcock's *Psycho,* before going on to write a "real" opera, *Wuthering Heights.* Even though his Brontë opera was a failure, Herrmann had the operatic knack for telling characterization. Take *Psycho,* for instance: can you conjure up a scene from the movie—Janet Leigh driving nervously through the rain with a sack of money in the trunk of her car, Martin Balsam creeping up the stairs to visit Mrs. Bates's bedroom and, of course, the famous shower scene—without hearing Herrmann's eerie music in your mind? Of course not.

The other great outlet for music theater talent in America was the Great White Way. What was the original version of Jerome Kern's *Show Boat,* based on Edna Ferber's novel, if not an opera—a big, sprawling, angry family saga that was later shortened and prettified for wider consumption? What was Gershwin's *Porgy and Bess,* which was first performed on Broadway? What was Leonard Bernstein's *West Side Story* or *Candide?* Stephen Sondheim's *Sweeney Todd?* Operas all—but "operas" in the sense we are using the term here. Not stuffy, mummified works of high culture performed before the bejeweled and bewigged at the Met, but popular theater that has outlasted its origins, just like . . .

Just like "real" operas. When Mozart wrote *The Magic Flute,* he didn't write it for the ages; he wrote it for money. *Success now* was the name of that tune, and he was gratified no end when it came. "I am but just returned from the opera," he wrote to his wife on October 7, 1791, just a few months before he died. "It was quite as full as ever. The duet, *Man and Wife,* etc., and the glockenspiel in Act I were encored as usual—the boy terzett in Act II in addition. But it is the evident *quiet* approbation which best pleases me! It is apparent that this opera is rising rapidly and steadily in estimation."

The moral of the story is simple. Opera is where you find it, be it in Greek myth or modern history, in the back alleys of Catfish Row, or on a stroll across Abbey Road. Music theater is not just for the moneyed, it's for everybody.

Even you. But you already knew that.

INTERLUDE: RICHARD WAGNER

What are we going to do about Wagner? Terrible man, terrific music. Can't live with him, can't live without him.

Composers generally fall into two categories: those with great natural talent, who may or may not eventually make something out of it; and those lacking in innate, God-given gifts who succeed by dint of sheer hard work. Mozart and Saint-Saens are examples of the former, Beethoven and Wagner patron saints of the latter. Current musical ethos, reflecting sturdy Protestant egalitarian thinking, tends to prize the strivers over the gifted; they, after all, had to try harder. And, in any case, American society remains suspicious of natural ability, preferring to seek empirical, environmental explanations for each and every difference among persons this side of blue eyes.

Which is why Beethoven, for example, is the democrat's delight, a musical Horatio Alger story. Wagner had even less talent than Beethoven—Beethoven, after all, was a genuine keyboard prodigy, whereas Wagner never did learn how to play an instrument very well. The greatest and most influential musician—in fact, it can be argued, one of the most influential people, period—of the late nineteenth century was essentially an autodidact. (On his deathbed, Wagner's grandfather heard the young man torturing a piano in the next room. "And they say he has talent," muttered the old man, speeding toward the grave.) He didn't even decide to become a composer until he was fifteen years old, after hearing performances of Beethoven's *Ninth Symphony* (a work that remained a talisman to him all his life) and *Fidelio*. The only professional musical instruction he had came from a few short sessions in 1831 with the cantor of the Thomaskirche (Bach's church) in Leipzig. So: an inspiring success story, right?

Well, no.

Wagner was a bastard—figuratively, certainly; literally, probably. In all likelihood, his father was Ludwig Geyer, an actor in Leipzig who was a great and good friend of his mother. Geyer, who may have been Jewish, married her after Friedrich Wagner died, soon after Richard's birth in 1813, and the family moved to Dresden, where Wagner polished the strong, Saxon accent that his contemporaries made such sport of. All his adult life, Wagner was a virulent anti-Semite; perhaps this was his Oedipal revenge.

Like most composers, Wagner was short—about five feet five inches tall. But he thought big. He took what he wanted—money, women, opportunity—whether it belonged to someone else or not. He ran up huge debts, and outraged every community he ever lived in. He didn't care a fig for what anybody else thought. Rules, whether social or musical, were for other people; Wagner ordered his own reality. He got mad King Ludwig II of Bavaria to become his patron and when that wasn't enough, he built his own theater in the sleepy Franconian town of Bayreuth and created his own quasi-religious cult. He had two children by Cosima von Bülow, Liszt's illegitimate daughter, while she was still married to her husband, Hans, and he to his first wife, Minna. He borrowed money and rarely repaid it.

In short, he raised hell. At one point he was even a wanted man—wanted by the state of Saxony for his activities during the anti-monarchial revolution of 1848, which swept Europe. Wagner was an inveterate pamphleteer and, under the influence of the anarchist Mikhail Bakunin, fired off a broadside: "I will destroy the existing order of things," he warned. In short order, he found himself a refugee, first with Liszt, his patron, in Weimar and then in a safe haven in Zurich, Switzerland, until the fuss died down. (He wasn't legally allowed back in Germany until 1862.) Later, he lived under King Ludwig's patronage in Munich, where several of his most important operas were premiered, and then in Bayreuth. He died in Venice in 1883, having retreated south for the winter.

Wagner's life was a peripatetic odyssey of jobs: music director in Magdeburg in 1834, where he met and married Minna Planer and wrote his second opera, *Das Liebesverbot* (The Proscription Against Love), based on Shakespeare's *Measure for Measure*, which failed. Earlier, he had begun but not finished an opera called *Die Hochzeit* (The Wedding) and in 1833 completed *Die Feen* (The Fairies), which remained unproduced in his lifetime. But that was the extent of his compositional apprenticeship.

After a stop in Königsberg, Kant's hometown in East Prussia (now a postwar spoil of the Soviet Union), it was on to Riga, where he conceived *Rienzi*, an opera about an ancient Roman tribune that became his first big international success. But the good Latvians did not take kindly to Wagner's radical plans for restructuring their musical life, and in 1839 he was fired. He and Minna headed for Paris, the operatic capital of the world and the home of the most eminent practitioner of grand opera, Giacomo Meyerbeer. Meyerbeer, a German Jew whose real name was Jakob Beer, had made his reputation with spectacles like *Robert le Diable*—Liszt made a barnburning transcription of themes from this opera, which features a ghostly chorus of lascivious, dead nuns rising from their graves—and *Les Huguenots*, and Wagner needed his help if he was to make an impression on Paris.

He got it, but nothing much happened; all his life Wagner hated poor Meyerbeer for, as he saw, not helping enough. Broke, the Wagners bottomed out, Richard working on *The Flying Dutchman*, until the word came from Dresden that *Rienzi* had been accepted for performance. It was a hit, and, by 1842, Wagner's reputation was made.

Throughout the *wanderjahre*, he never stopped writing. Came the operas based on Germanic myth: *Tannhäuser*, about a song contest on the Wartburg, the great castle that towers over the town of Eisenach, where Bach was born. *Lohengrin*, Wagner's first treatment of sacred redemption that found full flower in *Parsifal*. *Der Ring des Nibelungen*, the sprawling four-opera mythological epic that consists of *Das Rheingold*, *Die Walküre*, *Siegfried*, and *Götterdämmerung*. Between the second and third acts of *Siegfried*, Wagner took a ten-year break and wrote both *Tristan und Isolde* (having fallen violently in love with Mathilde Wesendonk, the wife of one of his Swiss patrons), and his only comedy, *Die Meistersinger von Nürnberg*.

Wagner worked like a dog. How did he find the time to not only write his operas—and their librettos—but to issue a steady stream of broadsides and letters, keep one step ahead of his creditors, and find time to chase other men's wives and travel across Europe repeatedly? Wagner was almost as important a philosopher as a musician—in his own mind, he *was* as important, if not more so (Nietzsche thought so, too)—and his theories ranged on everything from *The Art Work of the Future* (he was for it)—the famous *Gesamtkunstwerk* that combines music, drama, poetry, and myth in one glorious package—to his revenge on Meyerbeer, the notorious *Jewishness in Music* (he was against it). As Peter Viereck points out in his exemplary study, *Metapolitics: The Roots of the Nazi Mind*, Wagner's theories were very much a part of the intellectual climate of the time, and would find lethal expression in the deeds of a Wagner fanatic, Adolf Hitler, who declared: "Whoever wants to understand National Socialistic Germany must know Wagner."

In fairness to Wagner, he cannot be blamed for something that happened half a century later (there's the Historic Fallacy again)—and his avowed anti-Semitism did not prevent him from engaging Hermann Levi to conduct the premiere of his last opera, the ultra-Christian *Parsifal*—but it does account for why admiration for Wagner is always tempered by a kind of wariness. Even today in Bayreuth, Hitler's ghost is never very far away; Wagner's daughter-in-law, the English-born Winifred, was a close personal friend of the Austrian corporal, and after the war she was banned from having anything to do with the freshly denazified Wagner Festival.

But an even stronger ghost is Wagner's. It seems incredible, but the man who today runs the Wagner Festival, Wolfgang Wagner, is the *grandson* of a man born in 1813. Wagner's villa, Wahnfried (the name means "freedom from folly"), still stands, although it was severely damaged by bombing during World War II. The streets are named after members of the Wagner family and characters in the Wagner music dramas. There is even a "Parsifal-Apotheke," the Parsifal Drug Store. No composer in history had as audacious a vision as Wagner's and made it stick.

Why is his vision so powerful? Why does his music have the effect on people that it does? Wagner did destroy the existing order of things, only not quite the way he pictured during his days as a firebrand. He soon lost his revolutionary fervor, as far as politics were concerned, and soon enough was nattering about the "vulgar egotism of the masses." But he never forsook his revolutionary art. Wagner was the great poet of sex, the seeker after Goethe's Eternal Feminine, and his music seethes with desire and longing, the violent clash between the sexes, the final struggle between Eros and Thanatos. No wonder it makes people uncomfortable.

Almost from the beginning, opinion was sharply divided. The philosopher Friedrich Nieztsche was first an acolyte and then an enemy. In 1876, at the first performance of the *Ring* in Bayreuth, he wrote (in *Richard Wagner in Bayreuth*) that the *Ring* "contains the most highly moral music I know." Later (in his book *Human, All Too Human*), he called Wagner "a Romantic in despair, decaying and rotten." (A few months later, Wagner exclaimed to Cosima, "Everything that wicked man has comes from me, even the weapons he uses against me. How perverse he is, how cunning, yet how shallow!")

Another foe was the Viennese music critic, Eduard Hanslick, whose perceived small-mindedness and petty nitpicking Wagner lampooned as Beckmesser in *Die Meistersinger* (Wagner almost called the character Hans Lich). After the first performance of the *Ring* at Bayreuth in 1876, Hanslick cabled his opinion: "a distortion, a perversion of basic musical laws, a style contrary to the nature of human hearing and feeling. One could say of this tone poetry: There is music in it, but it is not music." Leo Tolstoy called the *Ring* "a model work of counterfeit art so gross as to be even ridiculous." More poetically, Debussy said: "Wagner was a beautiful sunset that has been mistaken for a sunrise."

Wagner's defenders, of course, are legion; they include Thomas Mann (who employed the Wagnerian leitmotif technique in his novels) and George Bernard Shaw (who wrote *The Perfect Wagnerite*), among many others. Virgil Thomson, the American composer and critic, observed that the very number of Wagner's enemies pointed to his influence. "Wagner's pretensions to universal authority are inadmissible from the very fact that the music world is not unanimous about admitting them," Thomson wrote in *Dissent from Wagner* (1943). "Mozart is a great composer, a clear value to humanity, because no responsible musician denies that he is. But Wagner is not an absolute value from the very fact that Rossini denied it, and Nietzsche denied it, and Brahms denied it, and, in our own time, Debussy and Stravinsky have denied it. This does not mean that, with the exception of Rossini, all these composers (including Nietzsche) have not stolen a trick or two from Wagner or accepted him as a major infuence on their style. They have. But the fact that they have accepted his work with reservations is what proves my thesis. . . ."

It has been said that more has been written about Wagner than about any other man who ever lived, with the exceptions of Napoleon and Jesus. Wagner was a man of such immense personal magnetism, such overweening ambition, such irresistible drive, that he took the nineteenth century by the throat and shook it until its brains rattled. Women made no secret of their attraction to him, crowned heads gave him money, an entire town willingly became his personal fiefdom.

Even today, the force of his blow is still being felt. The state of Wagner singing is constantly addressed, and fretted over. A new production of the *Ring* draws worldwide press coverage (and is impossible to get into). Books about him and his works are still published, studies of his techniques and influence continually being written. Cosima's diaries, two volumes of daily details of the Master's life from 1869 to 1883 (Cosima's diaries end the night before Wagner's death, and she never picked up a pen again in the forty-seven years of life—or professional widowhood—she had left), were issued in 1977 to wide acclaim. We have not yet lost our fascination with Wagner.

At the end of his life, Wagner was writing an essay on *The Eternal in the Feminine*, a subject that, in one way or another, is at the heart of all his major works. As he lay in bed, he spoke of the Rhinemaidens, the cause of so much grief in the *Ring*, and he remarked to Cosima, "I feel loving toward them, these subservient creatures of the deep, with all their yearning." He dreamed of receiving a letter from Mathilde, but in his dream did not open it: "What if Cosima is jealous?"

The next day, in his study, he skipped lunch to work on his essay. The last words he wrote were: "All the same, women's emancipation is proceeding only in an atmosphere of ecstatic convulsions. Love—tragedy." A massive heart attack felled him, the orgasm of death, and he died in Cosima's arms. She held him the rest of that day and all through the night. In the autopsy report, the attending physician noted, "It cannot be doubted that the innumerable psychical agitations to which Wagner was daily exposed on account of his particular mental outlook, his sharply pronounced attitude toward a whole series of burning problems in the fields of art, science, and politics, and his noteworthy social position, contributed much to his unfortunate end." He was 69.

Perhaps the last word on Wagner belongs to Nietzsche. "I can understand perfectly when a musician says today: 'I hate Wagner, but I cannot stand any other music,' " he wrote in *The Case of Wagner* (1888). "I would also understand a philosopher who said: 'Wagner summarizes the modern age. There is nothing for it—one has got to be a Wagnerian.' "

5

THE BASIC REPERTOIRE—AND BEYOND

You're finally ready. You've learned about symphonies and concertos and opera and chamber music. But you're tired of just hearing about these things. Now you're prepared to strike out on your own and actually listen to something.

So let's talk repertoire.

If this were a conventional guide, we'd start with Bach, Beethoven, and Brahms, go on to Dvorak, Elgar, Gluck, and Haydn, get to Ives, Kodaly, and Leoncavallo, etc. And then I'd give you record recommendations so you could head out with your shopping list and your shopping cart and buy up a storm.

But we're not. We're not going to do it that way at all.

I mean no laundry list. No pick one from column A and one from column B. No Chinese menu? What kind of a guide book is this, anyway?

It's one that's trying to encourage you to think for yourself. I could start with Johann Sebastian Bach and proceed to Alexander Zemlinsky, but it would be wrong. (Alexander Zem*who*sky, you wonder? Zemlinsky. He was Arnold Schoenberg's teacher and brother-in-law, who wrote deep dark late-romantic music that is really quite attractive.)

I could do that. But I won't.

Why not? Because it's boring, that's why. Boring for you, even more boring for me. Have you ever noticed that music critics, for some reason, are expected to hand out free opinions at the drop of a hat? Doctors call this a "curbside consultation" and they hate it, but I've got to tell you they are among the worst offenders. Just watch an M.D.'s eyes light up when he meets a critic at a party and slides over for a little shop talk. (Doctors and corporate takeover artists are about the only ones who can afford the expensive seats up near the front these days.) "Okay, doc, I'll tell you about the Met's new *Ring* cycle if you'll just have a look at this brachialis muscle here. Whaddya say? Deal?"

You're not a doctor. (You are? Oops!) And you're never too old. For proof, check out *Tone Deaf and All Thumbs?: An Invitation to Music-making* (published by Vintage), a nifty little volume by a San Francisco neurologist named Frank R. Wilson, who took up the piano after he saw his two daughters thriving on the instrument, and lived to give his first recital. ("Hey, doc, would you mind taking a look at my optic nerve? I think it's a little swollen.") Wilson's point is that we all have the ability to make music, and that we shouldn't be intimidated by any bogus mystique into thinking that performance is only for the godlike. Anybody can do it. Even you.

The purpose of this book is to get you to open your mind and your ears and start listening. Nobody listens anymore. But listening can be a very valuable experience. Think of it: you can actually learn something by listening. And by doing, of course. So let's start doing.

What I'm about to give you is very much a personal tour of the classical music horizon. What follows is a listing of basic works in the genres we have been discussing—symphony, concerto, opera, chamber music—that completely reflects my own tastes. As elsewhere, I make no pretense to objectivity or completeness in this list. No doubt I've ignored favorites, I've blatantly insulted great works and great composers, and I've discussed fringe pieces that would make most subscribers to the Friday afternoon philharmonic series stalk up the aisle in a huff. As Brahms once said, "If there is anyone here I have not offended, I deeply apologize." So let's go. Ready?

A HIGHLY OPINIONATED, TOTALLY ARBITRARY GUIDE TO THE BASIC REPERTOIRE
In Which the Listener Is Encouraged to Seek Further
Enlightenment
and Open New Vistas
by Using His or Her Head
and Imagination

Symphonies

BRAHMS: *SYMPHONY NO. 2 IN D MAJOR*
Anyone looking for the perfect introduction to the symphony should say hello to Brahms's *Second*. The image of the short gruff little guy with the big long beard and the big bad manners is so firmly engraved in our imaginations—Brahms as the Gloomy Gus of music—that it seems hard to believe that the Tiny Terror of Vienna could have written such a sunny symphony as the *Second*. From the romantic opening horn to the final blazing blast of the brass, the *Second* is Brahms's most satisfying work; to hear it played by a crack outfit like the Berlin Philharmonic under Herbert von Karajan is one of life's greatest pleasures.

Naturally, Brahms partisans will give you an argument on this one. All his life, Brahms was obsessed by the ghost of Beethoven, and he spent many long years and several false starts working on his first symphony—which was promptly dubbed "Beethoven's *Tenth*" by the conductor Hans von Bülow. With friends like that . . . And, in fact, the *First* does bear some resemblance to the works of its spiritual godfather; when someone pointed out that the big theme of the finale was strikingly reminiscent of the main subject of the finale of Beethoven's *Ninth Symphony*, the irascible Brahms snapped: "Any ass can see that!" And any ass could, too.

If the *First* is big and bold, the underrated *Third* is subtle and restrained; each of its four movements end quietly, which may account for its infrequence of performance in the concert hall; there is no big slam-bang ending for conductors to show off in. The *Fourth* is much admired by those who find the Phrygian mode and the passacaglia form of interest—the mode is an old-fashioned scale, minus the black notes; the passacaglia is a Renaissance musical form in which the bass line remains steady throughout the piece, sort of like a rock song—but I find the piece rather cold and disappointing.

The *Second*, however, is all glory and will put a smile on your lips and a spring in your step. If you like it, and have tried the other Brahms symphonies, you will want to move smartly along to the *Seventh Symphony* of Antonin Dvorak, as Brahmsian as all get-out. And for a fillip, check out Joachim Raff's spooky *Lenore Symphony*, a mid-nineteenth century piece that was much admired in its day, as was Raff. He was, in fact, considered the finest symphonist of the century—until Brahms came along and blew him away.

BRUCKNER: *SYMPHONY NO. 9 IN D MINOR*

Anton Bruckner was another short little guy, this time with baggy pants and a whiffle haircut and a bad Beethoven fixation—but, hey, the man *was* an organist. Bruckner was such a dweeb that he once tipped a conductor who premiered one of his symphonies, such a wuss that he let well meaning friends carve up his music in the interests of making it more playable (sometimes he carved it up himself), such a weenie that, despite the fact that most of his symphonies begin exactly like Beethoven's *Ninth*, he could not dedicate his *Ninth* to Beethoven. That would have been presumptuous. Instead, he dedicated it to God.

The *Ninth Symphony* is, to my mind, his finest work, even if it is unfinished (perhaps *because* it is unfinished, the uncharitable might suggest). Bruckner, who always did have trouble with finales, died before he could finish the fourth movement, but on his deathbed he suggested that his choral work, the *Te Deum*, be used instead. Now that really would have been a ripoff, because Beethoven had invented the concept of a choral finale in the *Ninth*;

that's why it is often referred to as the *Choral Symphony*, especially in Britain.

Is it possible that all Bruckner symphonies sound alike? Well, yes, they kind of do: a mammoth first movement, a radiant slow movement, a clunking scherzo that sounds like tanks trying to dance (sometimes the order of these two movements is reversed), and a diffuse finale that often reprises the theme of the first movement before it staggers to a close. Because it is missing its finale, the *Ninth* automatically goes to the top of the list; it ends with Bruckner's noblest utterance, the slow movement. The *Ninth* is a work so affecting that I spent the fall semester of my sophomore year in college listening only to it and the Vaughan Williams's *Pastoral Symphony* (No. 3).

If you like it, then I urge you to sample some of the others. The *Seventh* is a magnificent creature, ditto the *Eighth*. I wouldn't give you a nickel for the turgid *Fifth*, admired in Germany though it is, but an undiscovered treasure is the *Sixth*, the source of both the theme from the movie *Born Free* and, in the slow movement, *Somewhere* from Bernstein's *West Side Story*. It's also one of Bruckner's tighter symphonic arguments.

Some years ago, it was customary to lump Bruckner together with another late romantic symphonic, Gustav Mahler. You'll still see it in the old books: "Bruckner and Mahler," like a Viennese law firm. But not only were they completely different personalities, they also wrote completely different music; about the only thing they have in common is a post-Wagnerian sense of harmony. Bruckner was a humble peasant Catholic from Austria; Mahler was a hot-tempered Christianized Jew from Bohemia. Bruckner was obscure; Mahler, the director of the Vienna Opera and, later, the New York Philharmonic, was world famous. Bruckner you could trip over; Mahler you couldn't miss. A Bruckner symphony is a private communion with the Deity in church; a Mahler symphony is primal scream therapy at the analyst's. Any ass can hear that.

MAHLER: *SYMPHONY NO. 9*

In fact, try it for yourself. There are more popular Mahler symphonies—the *First*, which used to be called *The Titan* but for some reason doesn't seem to be anymore; the *Second*, which is still known as the *Resurrection;* the very lovely *Fourth;* even the *Fifth*, which boasts the very famous (and very sexy) Adagietto. There are bigger Mahler symphonies—the mammoth *Third*, whose opening movement lasts as long as most normal symphonies, and the *Eighth*, which is not called the *Symphony of a Thousand* for nothing. (The "thousand" refers to the ideal number of performers, although frankly I've always thought of it as the number of times you consider suicide as a viable alternative during its performance.)

If neurosis in music is your idea of a good time, then Mahler is your man; is it any wonder that Freud invented psychoanalysis just down the street? Like many maniacs, though, Mahler can be quite impressive when he gets rolling, and there are long stretches of the *Ninth* that are quite moving, especially the desolate finale, which makes the same movement of Tchaikovsky's *Pathetique Symphony* look like a Mozartean romp in the woods.

A word about the symphony's numbering. Mahler was superstitious (surprise!), especially about death (surprise, surprise!); when it came time for him to write his ninth symphony, he decided he would cheat the Grim Reaper by calling the piece *Das Lied von der Erde* (*The Song of the Earth*) instead. Having thus delivered a big curve while Death was looking for a fastball over the outside corner, Mahler went on to write this symphony. And you know what? He lived! Then he started his *Tenth Symphony*. And you know what? He died! (When you do hear the Mahler *Tenth*, it's in a performing version by someone else, often Deryck Cooke.) Final score: Death 1, Mahler 0.

BEETHOVEN: *SYMPHONY NO. 3* (*EROICA*)

You didn't think I'd ever get to Ludwig van, did you? I've chosen the *Eroica* not because it's his best symphony, which it is, but because it's the most important. You'll get an argument from supporters of the *Ninth* on this one (see above) but the *Third* is really the piece that kicked out the jams. Before the *Eroica*, the classical symphony was tooling along nicely on six cylinders, having achieved perfection under Mozart and Haydn. Then along came the ungainly, pock-marked oaf from Bonn, whose piano playing was so wild and crazy that he broke strings and pounded instruments practically into matchsticks. Well, he felt the same way about the symphonic form. After giving it a go in two really very nice works, the *First* and *Second* (the *First* is better), he blew it away with the *Third*.

How did he do it? First of all, the *Eroica* (the name means *Heroic* and the symphony was dedicated to "the memory of a great man," originally Napoleon, but Beethoven got cranky when the little Corsican upgraded himself from Consul to Emperor) was long—about twice as long as the usual symphony. Second, it had a funeral march for a slow movement (in 1803, Beethoven obviously knew something Napoleon did not). Third, it had a mammoth theme and variations for a finale, using a tune that Beethoven had employed earlier in a ballet called *The Creatures of Prometheus*. It set the world on its ear, and the symphony was never the same after that. Beethoven, either, for that matter: the *Eroica* is the work in which he invented himself.

MOZART: SYMPHONIES

Yes, all of them. Forty-one of them. On original instruments. You don't have to listen to all forty-one at one sitting. But have them there, by your side, and feel free to call on them whenever you need a friend.

A word about the symphonies (a book about the symphonies!). The hits tend to be back-loaded, and while you will want to try some of the early ones, you really shouldn't miss the *Haffner, Linz*, or *Prague* symphonies, or the famous last three symphonies in E-flat, G minor, and C major (the *Jupiter*). Please allow me to tip you off to the *Prague*, sometimes overlooked in the shuffle of its competitors, but one of Mozart's happiest creations nonetheless. Pay close attention to the closing theme of the first movement's exposition; never content to leave well enough alone, Mozart alters it subtly—but deliciously—when it returns at the end of the movement. You can enjoy the piece without noticing little details like this, but when you do, the frisson is all the greater.

In the old days—less than a decade ago—your choice of recorded Mozart was pretty much limited to the smooth, rounded school of conducting exemplified by Sir Thomas Beecham and Bruno Walter, or the even more smooth and rounded, if not to say treacly and enervated, leadership of Karajan. Bernstein was too vulgar, Maazel too cold, Ozawa too ham-fisted. Then came the original instruments movement.

It started in England. Small groups of players gathered to perform eighteenth century music on instruments of the period. "How would this have sounded in Mozart's day?" they wondered, and out came the gut-stringed violins and the wooden flutes. It was an outgrowth of the pioneering work done in medieval and renaissance music by such ensembles as Musica Reservata and Thomas Binkley's Studio der Frühen Musik in Munich, and it has had a profound effect on the way the music of this period is now viewed.

But it makes sense, doesn't it? A composer has the sound of the instruments of his day in his ear when he writes. Bach did not envision his organ music arranged by Leopold Stokowski and played in *Fantasia;* Beethoven could not have foreseen the modern concert grand piano.

It goes even further. Once I visited the Thomaskirche in Leipzig, the church where Bach spent many years as cantor. By chance, the organist was practicing a Bach toccata when I walked in, and as the last chord sounded, I had a startling realization: whether consciously or unconsciously, the performer had gauged his tempo to the church's reverberation time, so that the last overtones disappeared in time with the (now-unheard) rhythm. To really be authentic, in other words, we would have to hear music in its original venue.

That's obviously taking things too far. But a highly persuasive case is being made for adopting the instruments and the phrasings and the tempos of the music's period. It just sounds better that way. When British conductor Christopher Hogwood's complete cycle of the Mozart symphonies appeared on L'Oiseau-Lyre records, I hailed it as "one of the most important projects in the history of the phonograph." While it is now fashionable to compare Hogwood unfavorably to his colleagues Trevor Pinnock, Roger Norrington, and John Eliot Gardiner (Brits all), I still stand by my statement. You'll never want to hear Mozart any other way. If you do, there's always Bruno Walter.

MENDELSSOHN: *SYMPHONY NO. 4 (ITALIAN)*

As his name implies, Felix Mendelssohn was a happy guy. At least his music makes him seem that way. And there is no sunnier piece in the repertoire than the *Italian Symphony*, which you may recall from the film *Breaking Away*. The *Italian* is full speed ahead right from the get-go: the bouncing woodwinds, the surging strings, the leaping opening melody are all calculated to put a smile on your face. And, amazingly, it just keeps getting better.

Of the other Mendelssohn symphonies, my favorite is the *Fifth*, subtitled the *Reformation*. In it, you will hear the famous "Dresden Amen," a hymn cadence that Wagner later used to great effect in his last opera, *Parsifal*. The *Third Symphony*, called the *Scottish*, is also worth a listen. And don't forget the *Hebrides Overture*, better known as *Fingal's Cave*.

SCHUMANN: *SYMPHONY NO. 2 IN C MAJOR*

It's a cliché of music criticism that Robert Schumann was a composer whose gifts were best suited to the realm of piano and song; that his pushy wife, Clara, drove him to write symphonies; and that when he did he turned out to be an idiot at orchestration. Well, not quite right.

The *Second Symphony* is one of the best nineteenth century symphonies, offering an ineffable slow movement and a whirling scherzo that has some of the most exciting string writing in the literature. And the other three symphonies aren't bad, either. The *First*, called the *Spring Symphony*, leaps at you with horns blazing.

The *Third*, known as the *Rhenish Symphony*, has a famous musical portrait of the Cologne Cathedral. The *Fourth*, in D minor, is an enjoyable listen. Don't always believe what you read; with Schumann symphonies, hearing is believing.

BERLIOZ: *SYMPHONIE FANTASTIQUE*

This is a famous musical hard-to-believe: hard to believe that this daring, brilliantly orchestrated depiction of a drug addict's erotic hallucinations appeared in 1830, just three years after the death of Beethoven. Hector Berlioz was one of those rarities in the nineteenth century, a composer who was not a virtuoso on an instrument; his instrument was the orchestra, and he played it like a harp.

The key to understanding the *Fantastique* is Berlioz's use of the *idée fixe*, or recurring tune that in this case represents the Beloved. A girl has driven the young man crazy and he has overdosed on opium; the symphony is his nightmarish dream, in which she keeps reappearing. The most celebrated movements are the fourth (the March to the Scaffold) and the fifth (the Dream of the Witches' Sabbath), both hair-raising exercises in musical imagination. Listen particularly to how the *idée fixe* comes back in the finale; instead of a luscious vision of beauty, the melody is distorted into the shape of a crabbed old hag. Just keep telling yourself: it's only a symphony, it's only a symphony.

IVES: *SYMPHONY NO. 2*

What is Charles Ives doing in this illustrious company, you wonder. Or, maybe, *who* is Charles Ives, you wonder. "Are my ears on wrong?" Ives once wondered. "I'm the only one, with the exception of Mrs. Ives (and one or two others, perhaps), who likes any of my music. . . ." Not quite right, Charlie.

I like Ives's music and so will you—some of it, anyway. The *Second Symphony* is a good place to start. If you know anything about Ives, you probably know that he was a Connecticut Yankee from Danbury who made his fortune selling insurance in New York

City by day and, in near total obscurity, writing his dense, difficult music by night.

That's only half right. The biographical part is correct, but the pigeonholing of the music is not. True, Ives was a polytonal revolutionary—he loved the sounds of keys clashing, like armies in the night—and some of his best and most important works are uncompromisingly experimental. (Although he lived until 1954, he had stopped writing music around 1922, when he privately published a volume of 114 songs. His best works date from the period 1900–1910.) But he was also very interested in Americana, and his music positively bristles with nostalgic quotations from folk and popular music. Few composers evoke the spirit of the U.S. in the late nineteenth century better than Charles Ives.

The *Second Symphony* is in many ways his most accessible and representative composition. Don't worry about dissonance: except for one big moment, which I'll get to in a minute, it is a tune riot. "Columbia the Gem of the Ocean" (an Ives favorite), "America the Beautiful," and other well-known melodies rub shoulders with Ives's own big, broad-shouldered tunes, some of them achingly evocative of a vanished New England—the small-town America of village greens and Sunday socials and hymn tunes and Fourth of July fireworks. Because the *Second* is a relatively early work, it still reflects the influence of Ives's teacher at Yale, Horatio Parker, and, as in the *First Symphony*, there are echoes of Brahms and Dvorak in it.

About that dissonance. In the finale, Ives delivers a tremendous conclusion: "Columbia the Gem of the Ocean" is being belted out on the brass and the rest of the orchestra is going crazy when suddenly, as the movement comes to an exciting conclusion, it erupts in a tremendous raspberry, as if an Army bugler had gone horribly wrong on the last note of "Reveille." It's funny and shocking and exhilarating all at once. In other words, it's Ives.

If you find that the *Second Symphony* is your kind of music, then run, don't walk, down to the record store and get yourself a copy of the Ives *Piano Trio*. It's a little tougher than the *Second Symphony*, but it's the highest manifestation of Ives's kitchen-sink philosophy of composition. Don't be mystified by the enigmatic title of the second movement, TSIAJ. In a typically Ives bit of guying, it means, "This Scherzo Is a Joke" (*scherzo*, of course, being the Italian word for *joke*).

Of the orchestral music, the *First Symphony*, as we've noted, is fairly conventional, but attractive. The *Third Symphony* is a downright masterpiece, subtle and wonderful, while the sprawling *Fourth* has one of Ives's most beautiful moments, the slow movement, which Ives borrowed from one of his earlier string quartets. (If you don't write nine symphonies, like Beethoven, et al., then you write four, viz: Schumann, Brahms, and Ives.) And be sure to give *Three Places in New England* a listen, too; it contains one of the finest river portraits in all music—right up there with Smetana's *The Moldau*—in *The Housatonic at Stockbridge.*

Don't be put off by Ives's reputation as an ear-shattering primitive. You'll be glad you didn't.

SHOSTAKOVICH: *SYMPHONY NO. 15*

The *Fifth Symphony*, the work Shostakovich wrote to atone for his sins against socialist-realist sensibility, is the most popular work by the late Russian; the *Seventh*, known as the *Leningrad*, the most notorious. But the *Fifteenth*, his last, is to my mind the best introduction to the Shostakovich style. Not that it is the most typical; it begins with a quote from the *William Tell* Overture, and ends with a gloss on the Fate motif from Wagner's *Ring*. But all the characteristic Shostakovichian touches are here: the rattling snare drums, the swooping flutes and piccolos, the machine-gun string writing; the high spirits and the gloomy depths.

The symphony, premiered by the composer's son, Maxim, was a hit at its first performance in 1972. (Shostakovich died three years later.) "Shostakovich here has converted the wealth of his life experience into inimitable musical illustration," wrote *Pravda*, and that's no cheap Commie propaganda. Having made his peace with the Soviet system long ago—be sure to read the fascinating and moving book *Testimony*, Shostakovich's memoirs as dictated to

Solomon Volkov—Shostakovich wrote what is perhaps his most enigmatic work. Listen in particular to the finale, which ends with a prolonged, hushed, and spooky passage for percussion. It is one of the strangest farewells in the symphonic literature, an aural analogue to the mysterious smile that always seems to be playing around the composer's tight, thin lips. What's the joke? The joke's on us.

VAUGHAN WILLIAMS: *SYMPHONY NO. 5*

English music is treated as if it were the Toby jug of the literature. But, aside from the hookey they played between Henry Purcell in the late seventeenth century to Sir Edward Elgar in the late nineteenth, the English do have musical talent. Really, they do.

Ralph Vaughan Williams wrote . . . yes, nine symphonies. The *First*, called the *Sea Symphony*, is a big lusty choral work in the grand nineteenth century British singalong tradition. But where "Rafe" really got cooking was in the *Second*, known as the *London Symphony*, a marvelous sonic portrait of the English capital. The *Third*, called the *Pastoral Symphony*, is another glowing tone poem, while the *Fourth* (no nickname) is a brutal, dissonant venture across No Man's Land.

And so we come to the *Fifth*. This delicious piece uses material from Vaughan Williams's underrated opera, *The Pilgrim's Progress;* there is probably not a more contemplative, spiritual work written in the twentieth century, unless it is the same composer's *Fantasia on a Theme of Thomas Tallis.* When the pressures of modern times start to get you down, slip the old *Fifth Symphony* on the turntable and just watch the alpha waves cool out.

In fact, just about all of Vaughan Williams is a tonic for what ails you: the operas, which also include *Sir John in Love,* another treatment of Shakespeare's Plump Jack; the *Songs of Travel,* for tenor and piano; the *Serenade to Music,* for sixteen solo singers; *An Oxford Elegy,* one of the few successful works for speaker and orchestra; *The Lark Ascending,* for violin and orchestra. Go out and buy them all. You'll thank me.

ELGAR: *SYMPHONIES NOS. 1 AND 2*

Say hello to Sir Edward, children. Yes, he looks like Colonel Blimp or something out of Gilbert and Sullivan or maybe even Sherlock's Dr. Watson. But he was a great composer just the same. You'll probably try the *Enigma Variations* first, as well you should, but do graduate to the two—only two!—symphonies. The slow movement of the *First* is one of the glories of the late romantic orchestral literature and the finale's peroration, in which the main theme of the first movement comes blazingly back, is a definite high. The *Second* is a little thornier, but stick with it.

MESSIAEN: *TURANGALILA SYMPHONY*

Olivier Messiaen is one of music's great visionaries, a deeply religious French Catholic, an organist by profession, who creates magnificent sonic cathedrals in sound. This one's not for the squeamish. But if you'd like to see what the modern symphony orchestra can do with all the stops pulled out, then *Turangalila* is for you. (The title, by the way, is a combination of two Sanskrit words: *turanga*, which means flowing time, movement, or rhythm; and *lila*, love, sport, or the play of the gods.)

The symphony's program (that is, its story line or source of inspiration) is eclectic: Tristram and Iseult, mystic Catholicism, the myths of ancient India and Peru, the stories of Edgar Allen Poe. But you don't need to know any of this to appreciate the work's majesty and sincerity. It's in ten movements and lasts well over an hour, and the first time you hear it you will think I'm completely nuts. But let it grow on you.

One item of note about this work: Messiaen has long had a fondness for an instrument called the Ondes Martenot, which you may recall from its use by Maurice Jarre in the score for *Lawrence of Arabia;* it makes a weird, swooping noise much admired by movie music composers for science fiction movies.

Another item of note: if you think the idea of writing a symphony with a Sanskrit title is eccentric, consider Philip Glass's opera, *Satyagraha*, whose text is *entirely* in Sanskrit.

Concertos

TCHAIKOVSKY: *PIANO CONCERTO IN B-FLAT MINOR*

This is it. Ichiban. Numero Uno. The Big One. The initial failure of the Tchaikovsky Concerto—he wrote two more, but nobody ever talks about, or plays, them—is the stuff of musical legend, but the work won acceptance very quickly and today it is all but unavoidable. Pianists make reputations with it and contests are won with it—Vladimir Horowitz ran away from Sir Thomas Beecham in it at their joint debut in 1928, and Van Cliburn triumphed with it at the 1958 Tchaikovsky Competition in Moscow. Its treacherous, cascading runs and daring, thundering octaves—not to mention its immortal opening melody ("Tonight We Love"), which, incredibly, is never heard again in the piece—have made it an audience favorite, the musical equivalent of going to the circus to see if the lions finally eat the tamer.

Sometimes they do.

RACHMANINOFF: *PIANO CONCERTO NO. 3*
IN D MINOR, OP. 30

There is, by contrast, nothing artless about Sergei Rachmaninoff, the dour Russian expatriate memorably characterized by Stravinsky as "a six and a half foot tall scowl." While not exactly artificial, Rachmaninoff's music is carefully calibrated for maximum effect; like Mozart, he wrote his concertos for himself to play. Unlike Mozart, he didn't mind showing off.

Most folks prefer the *Second Concerto*, with its famous pop-music themes, but the *Third* is, in every respect, a better work: showier, more dramatic, more exciting. For my money, not even that biggest, baddest warhorse on the block, the Tchaikovsky *First Concerto*, can match the Rach 3 (as musicians call it) for sheer kinetic thrills as Sergei winds up for his closing Sunday punch in the finale, punctuated at its close by the Russian's drumbeat rhythmic signature: *Dum*-da-da-dum. (Translation: *Rach*-man-i-noff. Now you know how to pronounce his name as well.) Yeah!

If this kind of fireworks is your cup of *chai*, then have a look at Rachmaninoff's other three concertos. The *Second* we've already discussed. The *First* is an exuberant youthful work, not much heard; and the weird *Fourth*, which (believe it or not) includes a set of variations on *Three Blind Mice*, is almost never played. I like it, though. You could also profitably investigate the Rachmaninoff symphonies: the big, bold *Second* is everybody's favorite, but I rather admire the *Third*, another enigma. His best orchestral work is probably the *Symphonic Dances*, but a piece I really enjoy is the early symphonic poem *Prince Rotislav*, as melancholy as all get-out and just the thing for a long Russian winter's evening. No wonder Rachmaninoff moved to Beverly Hills.

LISZT: *PIANO CONCERTO NO. 1 IN E-FLAT*

So you want fireworks, do you? Here's the granddaddy of fire-breathers, the great Franz his own bad self, the king of Lisztomania, Hungary's favorite son (even though he never learned to speak Hungarian), the sultan of the boudoir, the Abbé of Rome: Franz Liszt. There is something about Liszt—his Byronic, golden boy appearance, his reputation as a Lothario and, most of all, his stunning virtuosity. Liszt (the Germanic family name was List, later Hungaricized to Liszt, although pronounced the same way) was the man who invented the public piano recital, and the first one to play the late Beethoven sonatas in public. Even today, his reputation is the one against which all others are matched. The very name Liszt means virtuosity.

The E-flat concerto is one of two; the other is in A major. Oddly, neither is very good—certainly not the equal of the solo piano music. Those elements of them that Liszt's contemporaries thought most daring—the one continuous movement structure, the use of the triangle in the scherzo of the *First Concerto*—we don't much care about any more. And in comparison with, say Rachmaninoff, even the storied piano writing seems a little tame. These are not really criticisms: Liszt, of course, could not have known a Rachmaninoff would come along (unless he *anticipated* Rachmaninoff!). So we just have to take the concertos as they are, much like Chopin's, which are even worse.

Strange that the two greatest pianists of the early nineteenth century should bat a combined 0-for-4 in the concerto department, but such is the Muse's little joke, I guess. A really bang-up reading of the Liszt E-flat can still raise the hair on the back of your neck. Any pianist who is any pianist has to test his or her mettle in the Liszt concertos, and audiences still seem content to pay good money to hear them try. You might want to, too.

BRAHMS: *PIANO CONCERTO NO. 2 IN B-FLAT MAJOR*, OP. 83

Brahms again. I have a soft spot for the grouchy old guy. His bark was worse than his bite, and in his music he hardly barks at all. The *Second Concerto* may be the greatest piano concerto of all time, a construct of such dazzling breadth and scope that you practically want to learn the piano just so you can play it (although, unless you're real good, you probably never will). This concerto is the musical equivalent of the Greeks at Thermopylae, if they had won: the soloist battles incredible odds, somehow managing to keep his head on his shoulders through a titanic first movement, a rock 'em-sock 'em scherzo, a radiant slow movement in which the piano must out-beguile the solo cello, and a playful, almost Mozartean finale. It's the ultimate test of pianistic mettle, not as flashy as the Rachmaninoff but brutally hard and emotionally exhausting.

Once you've got the *Second* under your belt, take a look at the *First*, an early work in D minor that was originally intended as a symphony until Brahms chickened out (it took him 15 years, and several false starts, to finally produce the *Symphony No. 1*). The slow movement of the *First* is a musical portrait of the great love of Brahms's life, Clara Schumann, who was the wife of his friend and mentor, Robert Schumann. Brahms's passion for Clara was one of the great unrequited (?) love affairs of the nineteenth century, a passion that mellowed with the passage of time (after Robert's death in 1856, Clara wore widow's weeds for the rest of her life—forty more years). It's a wonderful, romantic story and you may ignore the ugly rumors that the Schumanns' last child looked an awful lot like Brahms.

While we're on the subject of Brahms's concertos, I insist you also get to know the noble *Violin Concerto*, a piece that will suck you in right from the start with an expansive opening theme for the orchestra and a burst of virtuosity from the violin soloist. I know I said I wasn't going to recommend recordings, but in this case, I'm going to break my rule: beg, borrow or steal the Erica Morini or Henryk Szeryng versions. No modern fiddler has the chops or the guts to play it the way either of these two could. As far as the *Double Concerto* is concerned—a strange piece for violin and cello with orchestra that sounds better on paper than it does in the concert hall—you're on your own.

Speaking of the cello, no discussion of basic concertos would be complete without a mention of the World's Most Famous—and the World's Most Onliest—cello concerto: the *Concerto in B minor* by Antonin Dvorak. You know, the one Susan Sarandon is practicing in *The Witches of Eastwick* when that old devil Jack Nicholson comes along for a little private instruction. There *are* other cello concertos, of course—by Schumann, Prokofiev, Sir William Walton—but the Dvorak is the people's choice.

MOZART: *PIANO CONCERTO IN B-FLAT MAJOR*, K. 595

It is another cliché of music criticism that Mozart's piano concertos are the abstract equivalent of his operas, in which the piano substitutes for voice. Frankly, I've never quite bought this argument. Mozart's operatic genius was *e pluribus unum*—out of the many, one (like many of the Founding Fathers, Mozart was a Mason; he would be perfectly familiar with all the arcane symbols on the American dollar bill). In the piano concertos, it was the reverse: he takes what is essentially the most confrontational of musical forms—a single soloist against an orchestra—and evokes a world of different voices: from the one, many.

While partisans may hold out for the dramatic *D-minor Concerto*, K. 466, or the sunny *A-major Concerto*, K. 488, the B-flat gets my nod by virtue of its surpassing mastery of both form and inspiration.

If you can read music, look at a Mozart score and you won't believe how simple it looks on the page. It is the world's only friction-free music. There is no wasted motion, no excess baggage, nothing to impede its progress. When Hemingway defined courage as grace under pressure, he should have been thinking of Mozart.

BEETHOVEN: *VIOLIN CONCERTO IN D MAJOR*, OP. 61

And Beethoven again. As long as we're on the subject of violin concertos, this seems like a good time to mention Beethoven's best piece. I can already hear you screaming about the *Fifth Symphony* or the *Eroica*, but I mean it when I say that, to my taste, the lovely *Violin Concerto* is the big B's most satisfying work. When Beethoven isn't hectoring you, he can be a pretty pleasant guy—witness the *Pastoral Symphony*, the Sixth—and when he unbuttons his vest and takes off his starchy collar he is downright amiable. The fiddle concerto is relaxed, tuneful, playful and, in the slow movement, quite beautiful. You ask yourself: can this be the same guy who wrote the trio (the contrasting section) of the scherzo of the *Seventh Symphony*, perhaps the single ugliest piece of music composed in the nineteenth century? It just shows to go you.

Of the Famous Five—the piano concertos—I offer these observations. *No. 1 in C major:* pleasant. *No. 2 in B-flat major:* terrible. *No. 3 in C minor:* pretentious. *No. 4 in G major:* the best of the lot. *No. 5 in E-flat major,* the *Emperor:* not as good as its reputation. In the first movement of No. 5, there is a moment when the piano suddenly breaks into a scalar passage, running up and down the keyboard. One day, while I was listening to a recording of the *Emperor,* my mother asked me during this part: "Why is the pianist practicing his scales in the middle of the piece?" I had no answer for her then and I have none now.

Amazingly, Beethoven arranged the *Violin Concerto* for piano and orchestra. Yes, he did. It sounds much better on the violin.

PROKOFIEV: *VIOLIN CONCERTO NO. 1 IN D MAJOR*

But enough of lovely. When you pay good money to go hear Itzhak Perlman put bow hair to steel string, you want fireworks. I don't blame you. Part of classical music's great attraction is its physicality, the sense that one human being with superhuman fine-motor skills is doing a basically impossible thing very well, and we're along for the ride.

Sergei "Fingers of Steel" Prokofiev may seem just another unreconstructed Bolshevik to you, but believe me, the tall, balding Russian can really deliver the goods. His piano concertos are highly effective vehicles, especially the famous *Third Concerto* in C major, but his finest work remains the 1917 *Violin Concerto No. 1*, which is at once lyrical and, in its scherzo, blazing. All the tricks of the fiddler's trade are unleashed in this piece, including *pizzicato* (plucking the strings) and harmonics (touching the string lightly to produce a note two octaves higher; it sounds like whistling). The *First* is the fiddler's Fourth of July. Try it; you'll like it. I am less fond of the *Second*, in G minor, although it has its admirers.

TCHAIKOVSKY: *VIOLIN CONCERTO IN D MAJOR*
See comments about Tchaikovsky: *Piano Concerto in B-flat Minor*, above, and substitute "violin" for "piano."

BERG: *VIOLIN CONCERTO*
Oh, no; can it be? Yes! A twelve-tone violin concerto. Worse, a gorgeously beautiful twelve-tone violin concerto. Along with Anton Webern, Alban Berg was one of Arnold Schoenberg's disciples. Berg was a tall, handsome Austrian, a real late romantic. Nothing was more late-late romantic than Schoenberg's twelve-tone system (however "modern" it may still sound to our ears), and it fell upon fertile ground in Berg.

Unlike Webern, though, Berg retained many of his original romantic impulses. The *Violin Concerto*, written near the end of Berg's life (he died from complications of a bee sting), and intended as a requiem for young Manon Gropius, the beautiful daughter of the architect Walter Gropius and Alma Mahler Gropius (yes, Mahler's widow and the greatest arts groupie of all time), contains a Carinthian folk song, a quote from a Bach cantata, and is, when all is said and done, basically in the key of G Minor. Put that in your dodecaphonic pipe and smoke it, Arnold!

Like the greatest pieces of music, the Berg *Violin Concerto* sets and defines a mood—in this case, one of elegiac grief. Berg was something of a musical numerologist and cryptographer. The *Chamber Concerto*, one of his most impenetrable creations, is based on a numerological series; his *Lyric Suite* for string quartet is a frank description of his secret love for Hannah Fuchs-Robettin, with his and Hannah's musical initials intertwined again and again. But the *Violin Concerto* is an altogether more straightforward work, one whose pain and suffering can be appreciated by any listener, no matter how innocent of knowledge of Schoenberg's theories. It is one of the greatest twentieth century orchestral pieces. Don't miss it.

DVORAK: *CELLO CONCERTO*
ELGAR: *CELLO CONCERTO*

This about sums up the basic concerted cello repertoire. We discussed the Dvorak previously, so let's move right along to the Elgar, first performed in 1919 and the composer's last major work. This is one of the most heartrending pieces in music, a work so ineffably sad that it defies description. One of music's great powers is to give us the ability to see into the souls of people long dead; to get an idea of the impact World War I had on the European consciousness, just listen to the Elgar *Cello Concerto*. And weep. When you've dried your eyes, move on to the same composer's *Violin Concerto*.

Opera

BERG: *WOZZECK*

You knew we'd get to opera sooner or later. Most people start their opera listening with something simple, like Leoncavallo's *Pagliacci* or Puccini's *La Boheme*. Not me. *Wozzeck* was the first opera I ever heard, and to this day it remains the one I love best.

It's not a twelve-tone opera—only one of its scenes (Act One, Scene Four) is written with the twelve-tone method. It is, however, atonal; that is, without a formal tonal center. But, as I mentioned above, Berg was an arch-romantic, and tonality is never very far away in his music. At the climax of *Wozzeck*, premiered in December 1925, the opera finds itself in an unequivocal D minor.

The title is a typo. It should be *Woyzeck*, but a printer made a mistake and double-zed *Wozzeck* it has been ever since. The libretto is based on the play by the remarkable Georg Büchner (1813–1837), a precocious genius whose plays are striking for alienated, aphoristic outlook. The subject is soldier abuse, and it would scare Count Floyd: Wozzeck is harassed by his martinet Captain, tortured by the Doctor in quack medical experiments, beaten up by the priapic Drum Major and scorned by the slatternly Marie, the woman by whom he has an illegitimate child ("without the blessing of the church!" as the Captain reminds him). Eventually he loses his mind, stabs Marie to death, and drowns himself in a lake while trying to retrieve the incriminating knife. Pretty scary, huh, kids?

Well, that's opera for you. Berg's genius was to transform this quick-cutting, almost cinematic story, into a short work of incredible impact. The critic Ernest Newman spoke to *Wozzeck*'s appeal in a series of articles he wrote for the London *Sunday Times* in 1949: "The non-technical listener to the opera finds himself, perhaps for the first time in his life, taking a vast amount of non-tonal music and not merely not wincing at it but being engrossed by it. That simple fact is the true measure of Berg's achievement; whether the listener can account for his interest or not, the fact remains that he is interested in *Wozzeck* throughout, that he feels the music to be not only 'right' for the subject but the only musical equivalent conceivable for it.

"Everything about *Wozzeck* is amazing."

Powerful too. Even today, patrons of the Metropolitan Opera stream out during a performance of *Wozzeck*, perhaps because Berg's unprettified music wedded to Büchner's potent play makes them just plain uncomfortable; it's so much easier when people are killing each other bloodlessly to the organ-grinder strains of Verdi. But you are made of sterner stuff. Buy the record (I like the Boulez recording, even with the inadequate Marie.) Block off three hours of your time. Unplug the phone and put out the cat. Then settle back with the libretto and follow along. Warning: Do not put on *Wozzeck*—or, indeed, any other piece of music you don't know by heart—as background music and expect yourself to absorb it. You must be an active listener; believe me, your activity will be amply repaid.

Ten years later, Berg wrote another opera, *Lulu*. Like *Wozzeck*, it is a sordid slice of life based on a play; in this case, two of them by the Austrian playwright Frank Wedekind (the late Louise Brooks played Lulu on film during her heyday in the German silent cinema). Unlike *Wozzeck*, it is a twelve-tone work, long, dense, and difficult. I love it very much, but I'd be remiss not to share with you Henry Pleasants's comment in his book *Serious Music—and All That Jazz!*: "I've always been put off by those critics who can speak of Strauss's *Ariadne auf Naxos* and *Capriccio* as Mozartean [they are], who find Nono and Dallapiccola 'lyrical' [they most certainly are], who can take seriously the pseudo-psychopathic nonsense of *Lulu* [I do]." Yo, Henry—lighten up!

SHOSTAKOVICH: *LADY MACBETH OF MTZENSK*

If you find that you like Berg, there are a number of other modern operas you will want to investigate. Foremost among them is Shostakovich's *Lady Macbeth of Mtzensk*, the piece that so frosted Stalin that it nearly cost Shostakovich his life. This tale of marital infidelity and murder in Old Mother Russia is one of the frankest examinations of sexuality in all opera. Despite Stalin's denunciation of "Muddle Instead of Music"—the title of the editorial in *Pravda* that condemned the piece in 1936—*Lady Macbeth* is composed in an accessible idiom. There are few operatic arias to equal the heroine Katerina's soliloquy in the first act, just before Sergei comes into her bedroom and violently seduces her. Talk about the calm before the storm: locked in a loveless marriage, the hot-blooded Katerina muses, "The foal runs after the filly/the tomcat seeks the female,/The dove hastens to his mate,/But no one hurries to me." And then, bang!

There is another magical moment in *Lady Macbeth*. When the drunken peasant stumbles into the cellar and discovers the body of Katerina's husband, Zinovy, the orchestra suddenly explodes with one of those patented Shostakovichian outbursts, all rippling snare drums and blasting brass, a chorus of triumph and terror, of shock and fear and high spirits. No one has ever depicted more vividly a hysterical nervous breakdown in music. This is the kind of music that makes dictators very, very nervous. No wonder it drove Stalin nuts.

MOZART: *THE MARRIAGE OF FIGARO*

Absolute monarchs seem to have trouble with revolutionary music, no matter what their political stripe. When Mozart's *Figaro* was premiered at the Imperial Court in Vienna, the Emperor was supposed to have remarked, "Too many notes, my dear Mozart, too many notes." To which the cheeky Salzburger replied, "But not one more than necessary, Your Highness." No wonder he had trouble getting a job.

And *Figaro* was revolutionary. It was based on the Beaumarchais play, a thinly disguised humorous gloss on the conditions that soon would lead to the French Revolution. Just three years after *Figaro*'s premiere in 1786, a lot of European crowned heads were waking up in the morning making sure that both head and crown were still attached to their bodies. It was also Mozart's first opera with Lorenzo da Ponte, the rogue Italian Catholic priest (converted from Judaism!) who worked with many of the great composers of the day (including—horrors!—Salieri) and who ended his days in Manhattan teaching Italian at Columbia University(!); he is buried in New York.

With *Figaro*, the history of modern opera begins. Certainly, the standard operatic repertory starts with it; while other works, including Mozart's own *Abduction from the Seraglio*, predate it, none is as frequently performed. The story of the wily servant Figaro's attempts to foil his lecherous boss's scheme to sleep with

Susanna on her and Figaro's wedding night—the old *droit de seigneur* gambit—is at once a metaphor for social oppression and a deeply human comedy whose tunefulness no one can resist. (Beaumarchais wrote three *Figaro* plays, and Mozart set the second of them. The earlier play, *The Barber of Seville*, was later put to music by Rossini as a kind of "prequel" to *Figaro*. The third play, *La mere coupable*, has not so far found its way into the opera house, although the American composer John Corigliano has been commissioned by the Metropolitan Opera and it may someday be performed.)

Certainly, a knowledge of *Figaro* is fundamental to understanding opera. Before it, there was nothing to equal the beauty of its arias, the brilliance of its ensembles, the poignancy of its sentiment and the hard, cold truth of its moral. Mozart's subsequent operas—the dashing *Don Giovanni* and the intricate *Così fan tutte*, both with da Ponte; *The Magic Flute* and the throwback *La Clemenza di Tito*—each have much to recommend them, of course. Many believe *Don Giovanni* to be the greatest opera ever written (although Beethoven, that old fart, thought the subject immoral); *Così*, too, has its partisans, myself among them. And nobody doesn't like *Flute*. But *Figaro* reigns supreme. Just listen to the end of the first act, to *Figaro*'s infectious marching song, and you'll know why.

PUCCINI: *LA BOHEME*

Speaking of marches, there's a nice one at the end of Act Two of *La Boheme*, the world's most romantic opera. (Why do you think they used it in *Moonstruck?*) It comes when Rodolfo, Mimi, and the other Bohemians have gathered at the Café Momus in Paris; there, Marcello has encountered his old flame Musetta, who is being wined and dined by one of her gentlemen callers, Alcindoro, and their love rekindles spontaneously. As a military patrol marches by, the fun-loving Left Bankers stride out with the troops, sticking the old duffer with the bill for all their meals. It's a moment of good times and high spirits, neatly offsetting the tragedy to come.

Many commentators have pointed out what a sadist the dapper, cigarette-smoking Puccini was: he loved to torture his heroines. Mimi dies of consumption. Tosca throws herself off the Castel Sant' Angelo. Madame Butterfly commits suicide; so does Liu, the spurned retainer, in *Turandot*. But Puccini understood something that a later generation of Hollywood B-movie makers would also grasp: the public loves a pretty girl in danger.

And Puccini colors the danger so nicely. His lovers are ardent, even when they are beastly; Lieutenant Pinkerton is a cad of the first water, but his love duet with Cio-Cio San in *Butterfly* is one of the glories of the literature. Prince Calaf is just as bad to Liu, but his aria "Non piangere, Liu" (Don't cry, Liu) is irresistible. Although Puccini was a composer of enormous sophistication—something his critics don't always realize, although they should just look at one of his scores—he relied on the musician's oldest and most invincible weapon to make his point: melody. He had a million of 'em.

VERDI: *DON CARLOS*

So, as you know, did Verdi. The trouble with Verdi for me, though, is his very high ratio of duds to hits. He once referred to *Aïda*, a dreadful piece of work, as his "least bad opera." Not quite right, Giuseppe. The Squire of Sant' Agata was being facetious, of course, although he was closer to the truth than he knew. Verdi's overall reputation is one of the great public relations jobs of all time—the greatest composer of the late nineteenth century, the operatic equal of Beethoven, etc., etc.

But have you ever heard, or heard of, the following operas: *Oberto, Un giorno di regno, Nabucco, I lombardi, Ernani, I due Foscari, Giovann d'Arco, Alzira, Attila, Macbeth, I masnadieri, Jerusalem, Il corsaro, La battaglia di Legnano, Luisa Miller, Stiffelio?* Yes, friends, they were all written by Verdi in the twelve years before he managed to get opera more or less right with *Rigoletto* in 1851. No wonder Verdi referred to most of this period as his "galley years"; you'd have to be a galley slave to listen to them.

Granted, once Verdi got rolling he did pretty well, although there are amazing lapses like *Il Trovatore*, perhaps the worst opera ever written by a major composer, and the aforementioned *Aïda* (*not*, by the way, written for the opening of either the Suez Canal or the Cairo Opera House). Verdi is often congratulated for the achievement of his later years, specifically the two operas he wrote on Shakespeare plays with libretti by Arrigo Boito, *Otello* and *Falstaff*. But the former appeared in 1887, the latter in 1893; after a half-century in the theater you would think he'd learned *something*.

Whatever the case, don't let me sour you on trying Verdi's indubitable masterpiece, *Don Carlos*. Originally, Verdi wrote the piece for the Paris Opera, in those days the mecca of operatic endeavor and the place where every composer coveted a success. The Opera was the grandest house in Europe, with the finest resources; a commission was highly sought after. Even so, the experience was not entirely a happy one for Verdi. The five-act opera was cut substantially even before opening night in 1867 (when it was, of course, sung in French), and on the whole it was not the smash hit Verdi had hoped for. The French drove him crazy, too. Back home in Italy some years later, *Don Carlos*, with the final "s" dropped, was revised, cut down to four acts (the first act was simply eliminated, with its tenor aria retrieved and inserted elsewhere in the opera) and turned into *Don Carlo*—the form in which it was known for most of this century.

Pound for pound, *Don Carlos* has more memorable moments than any other Verdi opera. The *auto-da-fe* scene, in which Philip II burns the Spanish heretics at the stake, is one of Verdi's most accomplished crowd scenes; Philip's anguished aria at the opening of the fourth act, when he realizes that his wife has never loved him; the chilling scene that follows with the Grand Inquisitor. Except for *Otello*, which has Shakespeare on its side (although the *Don Carlos* libretto is based on Schiller's play), Verdi never wrote a more human, gripping opera. In its epic sweep, poignant personal detail, sharply drawn characters and sophisticated musical settings, it is Verdi's finest work. *Don Carlos* is enough to make you forgive Verdi anything—maybe even *Alzira*.

Alas for perfection, the ending is marred by a ridiculous *deus ex machina*—old Charles V (or is it his ghost?) suddenly appears and pulls his grandson to safety (or is it the next world?). Nobody really knows what happens at the end of *Don Carlos*—it's a little like the end of *The Big Sleep*—but it's exciting and the crowd loves it. Of course, it wouldn't be Verdi if there weren't one astonishingly vulgar moment and Verdi delivers with the most banal marching tune imaginable in the *auto-da-fe*. (One of his biographers calls it the worst tune he ever wrote, which is saying something.) The march sounds like something they might have played at a Sicilian funeral a hundred years ago. But such is Verdi's overall brilliance in *Don Carlos* that, in this case at least, we can forgive him. Thanks, Joe.

MUSSORGSKY: *BORIS GODUNOV*

Here's another big, sprawling historical opera about real people, and another one of the glories of the operatic literature. Modest (that's his first name, not a descriptive adjective) Mussorgsky may have been a drunk, but he was a hell of a composer—amazingly, a favorite of Debussy, although their music has nothing in common—and a musician of audacious, original gifts. In *Boris,* Mussorgsky created the Russian national epic, even better than his colleague Alexander Borodin's *Prince Igor. Boris* has it all: imperious czars, scheming Polish plotters, false Dmitris, cunning peasants and sagacious monks, milling crowds outside the Kremlin, even a fool who weeps for Mother Russia at the end. Few sights in opera are as impressive as some gigantic Finnish bass (the only ones who seem up to the title role these days) toppling down the royal stairs near the opera's chilling conclusion.

Like the Bruckner symphonies, Mussorgsky's operas have been subjected over the years to the editorial emendations of various hands. Mussorgsky's tippling didn't allow him high marks for neatness or completeness, and his bull-in-a-china-shop originality meant that his radical first version of *Boris* was naturally rejected by the Imperial Theaters in St. Petersburg in 1871—at which point Mussorgsky thoroughly revised the piece, adding the love story between the Polish princess and the False Dmitri, among other things, to make it more palatable.

But both versions are splendid. So, naturally, Rimsky-Korsakov took it upon himself after Mussorgsky's death to clean up and reorchestrate *Boris*—twice. For years, the opera was known basically in the flashy, second Rimsky version, but lately scholars have succeeded in reawakening interest in Mussorgsky's originals. In 1940, Shostakovich also made a version of *Boris*, which is rarely heard, and Karol Rathaus prepared an edition for the Metropolitan Opera in 1952–53. You are still mostly likely to encounter the Rimsky version on records, and there's nothing wrong with it.

If you learn nothing else from *Boris*, I guarantee that you will learn at least one word of Russian: "Slava." Da!

About the other Mussorgsky operas, such as *Khovanshchina:* don't ask.

BRITTEN: *DEATH IN VENICE*

The safe pick to represent Benjamin Britten would probably be his first great opera, *Peter Grimes*. But *Death in Venice,* based on the Thomas Mann novella, is better—more daring, stranger, and ultimately more affecting. Britten's homosexuality was no secret, but in his last major work he faced up to it squarely; clearly, he saw something of himself in the character of Aschenbach, the German writer who ventures south to Venice, pederasty (implicit), cholera, and death.

Britten may be best known to the general public as the composer of the delightful *Young Person's Guide to the Orchestra,* which is really just a narrated version of his splendid *Variations on a Theme of Purcell*. But he was a great composer of vocal music—the *Serenade for Tenor, Horn and Strings,* written for his long time great and good friend, Peter Pears, and the magnificent *Les Illuminations,* based on poetry of Rimbaud, are just two of his masterworks in the genre. The many choral works, including the moving *War Requiem,* also ought to be mentioned.

And then there are the operas. Not just *Grimes,* but the gay comedy *Albert Herring,* the emotional *Billy Budd,* the chilling *The*

Turn of the Screw—say what you will about his music, but Britten's taste in literature was impeccable. But *Death in Venice* holds pride of place, for the imagination of its writing, for the way it captures the seductively degenerate spirit of Mann's book, and for the deeply human resonance the composer brings to what is for many an unsavory subject. Be sure to get to know it. Just don't tell your mother what it's about.

JANACEK: *JENUFA*

Another Slavic masterpiece, this one by Leos Janacek, one of the odder composers to strut across the operatic stage. Janacek was a funny looking guy who, like Verdi, wrote his best music at a rather advanced age. He spent a decade writing *Jenufa*, his first master-piece; when it was finished in 1904, he was already 60 years old. Janacek was a passionate Czech nationalist, so patriotic that he refused on principle to set foot in Prague's German-speaking theater. The Prague premiere in 1916 of *Jenufa* finally brought him fame outside his native province of Moravia, where he was known primarily as an instrumental and choral composer and director of the Organ School.

Janacek's operas—two other, later masterpieces are *Katya Kabanova* and *From the House of the Dead*—are acquired tastes, no doubt about it. Not because they are exceptionally dissonant, or atonal. No, they are very tonal; they even have hummable melodies. But the man simply was not of this earth when it came to his harmonic rhythm; that is, the pace at which the harmony changes under the melody. This may partly be due to the accents of Czech, which are very foreign to most Westerners, but even more to the accents of Janacek, which were Martian. "The art of dramatic writing is to compose a melodic curve that will, as if by magic, reveal immediately a human being in one definite phase of his existence."

Such curves! Janacek favored frank, even brutal subjects. In *Jenufa* a poor peasant girl gets impregnated by a local rowdy named Steva who happens also to be her cousin. The shame is so great that her foster mother, the Sextoness (called the Kostelnicka), drowns the infant in a handy nearby river. (In one sense, the opera is partly about this character; in fact, its real title is *Her Foster-Daughter*, the "her" referring to the Kostelnicka.) In the end, Steva's half-brother, Laca, marries a disfigured Jenufa, who rises above the village small-mindedness to achieve a human apotheosis.

For a close encounter of an orchestral kind, be sure to try Janacek's booming *Sinfonietta*. The tiny little title gives no hint as to the majesty and might of this music. Turn it all the way up when you listen to it. But make sure the neighbors have gone to Hawaii.

WAGNER: *DIE MEISTERSINGER VON NÜRNBERG*

Wagner wrote a comedy. Yes! Well, sort of. Not funny, you say? That's funny, I always thought . . . Maybe you're right.

The words *Wagner* and *funny* don't seem to fit together very well. *Post-funny*, maybe. What's funny about an opera in German that lasts five hours, whose humor, such as it is, is based on word play incomprehensible to 99.9 percent of audiences outside Germany and whose central character is—hold your sides—a shoemaker-poet named Hans Sachs?

Here's the secret: it's not that kind of comedy. More like a comedy of manners, a human comedy. In his other works, Wagner wrote about gods, dwarfs, dragons, flying Dutchmen, magic potions and Holy Grails, but in *Die Meistersinger*—the title means "The Mastersingers of Nuremberg"—he wrote about people, and that's why we love it so much. *Die Meistersinger* is about young love and the springtime, about an older man realizing he cannot have a younger woman, about the well deserved comeuppance of a crank (Wagner based this character, a carping snipe named Beckmesser, on his *bête noire*, the Viennese music critic Eduard Hanslick), and about the joy of a young man's coming of age. A fresh, genial wind blows through *Die Meistersinger*, one we don't often encounter in the gales that whistle through the *Ring* cycle or *Tristan und Isolde*.

Still, it's a tough nut to crack. I remember the first time I heard *Die Meistersinger*, on the radio (the worst place to encounter a new opera), and I thought it was boring. The experience so soured me that it was years before I finally came around. Probably the first thing about *Die Meistersinger* that you know is the famous Overture, but this is a good example of how misleading an orchestral excerpt can be, especially in Wagner. In the concert hall, the music ends with a great, final C major chord: so far, so conventional. But in the opera house, it segues directly into a magnificent chorale—the first scene takes place in church—and words literally cannot describe the chill that will rocket up your spine when you hear this effect for the first time.

Nuremberg has achieved a grim, posthumous reputation as the site of the war crimes trials after World War II; before that, it was where Hitler enjoyed staging his Hollywood-spectacular rallies, captured so brilliantly on film by Leni Riefenstahl in *Triumph des Willens*. But to the Germans, Nuremberg evokes the narrow, cobblestoned streets of Old Germany, whose gabled houses lurch into the alleys like weekend drunks, and where the night watchman made his comforting round to assure the citizenry that, for that evening at least, all was well with man and God.

It is this romance that colors every note of *Die Meistersinger*. Wagner was a great German patriot—even if he was a socialist revolutionary during the uprising of 1848—and as he got older he got more nostalgic for a Germany that even back then never really was. (Read an account of the unbelievable horrors of the Thirty Years' War to see how peaceful old Nuremberg was the century after the historical Sachs.) He was also fascinated by the German musical guilds of the Middle Ages, the Minnesingers (whom he wrote about in *Tannhäuser* and the Meistersingers. In *Die Meistersinger*, he used the strict rules of medieval composition (at least as he imagined them) to make a point about the dangers of stultifying orthodoxy. Even after he became the grand old man, strutting around Haus Wahnfried, his villa in Bayreuth, clad in silk underwear, he remained at heart a firebrand.

Which is why, I think, we forgive him so much. "Wagner has his moments—and his long half hours," a wag once remarked, and it's true that sometimes you have to wade through some fairly turgid passages before you get to the promised land on the other side. But get there you do; the Wizard of Bayreuth was a master craftsman and a man of the theater, who knew how to send 'em home humming. We just can't resist the old devil.

BIZET: *CARMEN*

Wagner was the eight-hundred-pound-gorilla of the nineteenth century; he picked his own seat and everybody else had to make do. Composers defined themselves by whether they accepted or rejected the tenets of Wagnerism. The philosopher Nietzsche was at first attracted to and then repelled by Wagner's ethos; he even wrote a book, *The Case of Wagner*, lambasting his former idol. (Wagner tends to have a religious effect on people; even today, his diehard followers are among the weirdest people you will meet in music. Some of them still refer to him as The Master. Really, they do.)

What's all this got to do with Bizet, you wonder? A lot. Nietzsche thought Bizet's masterpiece, *Carmen*, the greatest opera ever written, a healthy evocation of the vital, sunny south, in contradistinction to the neurotic, inward-looking, Germanic Wagner. Certainly, *Carmen* does seem to sum up all that is seductive about the transalpine culture, and in the gypsy girl we have a heroine who acts not according to predestined rules a la the characters of the *Ring*, but according to her own libido. No wonder Nietzsche loved her.

Carmen is a great opera, far better than its closest rival in the popularity contest, *Aïda*, and superior even to *La Boheme*, if only for its freshness (Puccini always seems more than a little calculated). Has there ever been an opera with more hit tunes than *Carmen*? From the infectious opening overture to its last anguished moment, *Carmen* brims with inexhaustible melody—an astonishing achievement from Georges Bizet, who, dead at 36 never got to savor his triumph. At its premiere at the Opera Comique, *Carmen* was condemned for an "obscene" libretto (it is based on the gritty novella of Prosper Merimee) and its music derided by critics as erudite, obscure, colorless, undistinguished, and unromantic. Which just proves that anybody can goof. As Mayor Fiorello

LaGuardia once said, "When I make a mistake, it's a beaut!" That didn't do poor Bizet any good; depressed from his opera's reception (who wouldn't be?), he fell prey to an attack of quinsy three months after the premiere. Two heart attacks finished him off.

Much ink has been spilled, and many trees slain, debating whether *Carmen* is really Spanish. Who cares? As we've noted elsewhere, the French had a monopoly on "Spanish" music in the nineteenth century; you might as well ask whether *Carmen* is really Jewish, since Bizet was. The point is *Carmen* is a masterpiece— the purest expression of melody wedded to the keenest psychological insight of any opera ever written. Yes, the librettists (including Bizet's father-in-law, Ludovic Halévy) prettified the story a bit with the sop Micaela, the girlfriend from home. But the music, for all its melody, keeps the raw edge of Merimee; that's what makes it so disquieting. We watch Carmen go to her doom over and over again; like Don Giovanni at the end of Mozart's opera, she spits in the eye of death and refuses to change her ways. There is a nobility in going down with the ship, as sea captains know, and both the Don and the Gypsy have it—in spades. In Carmen's case, hearts, clubs, and diamonds, too.

ORFF: *DER MOND*

Who's Orff? (Who's Yehudi?) Orff is Carl, the Munich-born composer whose music embodies the spirit of Bavaria. It may seem idiosyncratic of me to include an Orff opera at this juncture, but I think you could do much worse than to listen to *Der Mond* (The Moon), Orff's delightful fable of four friends who steal the moon from a neighboring village, take it to the afterlife, and draw the wrath of St. Peter. Orff, best known for the choral work *Carmina Burana*, lived forever (1895–1982) and while he remains something of a minority taste, had a profound effect on the course of modern music—specifically, minimalism.

Der Mond is a feel-good opera, folksy in its material, gentle in its story; the final image, of a little child looking up at the sky and exclaiming "There's the moon!" after St. Peter puts it back in the sky, as the zither softly strums in the background, sums up all that is right about Germany. You can safely avoid *Die Kluge*, a companion fable about a wise woman, but after you cut your teeth on *Der Mond* you might want to try Orff's *Antigonae* and *Oedipus der Tyrann*. Far from folksy, they are stripped-down, brutal treatments of Greek myth, raw and urgent.

BARTOK: *DUKE BLUEBEARD'S CASTLE*

No discussion of modern opera would be complete without a mention of Bela Bartok's *Bluebeard's Castle*, a one-act work of genius that I cannot recommend too highly. Although the thought of Bartok probably terrifies you, *Bluebeard's Castle* is a moody, mysterious work that treats the story of the sanguinary duke and his multiple wives metaphysically. The opening of the famous doors is a progression through Bluebeard's soul from riches to empire to the heart of darkness. At the fifth door, the curious Judith discovers Bluebeard's empire and the orchestra erupts with an enormous sequence of chords that suggest infinity. Then, at the sixth door, she finds the Lake of Tears; finally, at the seventh, she encounters his other wives and must solemnly take her place among them.

Bartok lavished some of his most beautiful and moving music on this short opera, overlaid with a characteristic Hungarian topspin. There is no better introduction to his music, or for that matter to twentieth century music, than this great masterpiece. Some windy fall night, when the leaves are swirling in the streets outside and the first chill of winter is in the air, kick back by the fireplace with a cognac, turn off all the lights, and give a listen to *Bluebeard's Castle*. You won't be sorry.

If you like *Bluebeard*, then by all means please listen to Luigi Dallapiccola's one-act, twelve-tone opera from 1950, *Il prigioniero*. If Berg hasn't convinced you that serial music can sing, Dallapiccola will.

A final word about opera. I promised you this list would be idiosyncratic and it is, skewed in favor of twentieth century works. Why? Because anyone can find his way to Bellini's *Norma* (a work, and a composer, I loathe) or to Verdi's greatest hits, or to, God knows, *Cav 'n' Pag*, opera's Bobbsey twins (*Cavalleria Rusticana* by Mascagni and *Pagliacci* by Leoncavallo, two one-acters generally performed together). But we're not interested in conventional wisdom here, except insofar as it is wrong. My job is to get you to enjoy music, not appreciate it. Trust me.

And now a word about Broadway. For some unfathomable, inexplicable reason, Broadway musicals have become the province of the people perhaps least qualified to write about them—the drama critics. Show me a drama critic who knows a thing about musicals and I'll show you a music critic, someone who regularly covers an art form that combines drama, singing, and dancing. That art form, as you should know by now, is opera. And so are some Broadway musicals.

Porgy and Bess began its life on Broadway. So did Leonard Bernstein's *Candide*. Believe it or not, Benjamin Britten's first opera, *Paul Bunyan*, was conceived for Broadway. And what are Sondheim's *Sweeney Todd* and Lloyd Webber's *Phantom of the Opera?* The trouble with the Broadway musical is Gresham's Law of the bad driving out the good or, in this case, driving them into the opera house. Anyone for *Romance, Romance?*

KERN AND HAMMERSTEIN: *SHOW BOAT*

For years, I labored under the misapprehension that this one was basically "Ol' Man River" and nothing more, a Hollywood operetta about frolicking white folks and suffering black folks, as content-free as *Brigadoon* and even more boring. How wrong I was!

The 1988 EMI recording, with opera stars Teresa Stratas and Frederica von Stade, opened my ears. Here is a score of raw power and urgency, written along frankly operatic lines: a surging opening chorus, a glowing tenor aria ("Who Cares?") radiant love duets ("Make Believe" and "You Are Love," and, of course, the great baritone aria with chorus, "Ol' Man River"—perhaps the finest song ever written by an American. True, the piece does run out of steam in the second act (the same criticism could be made of *Così fan tutte*) and not every tune is a winner. But who's counting?

BERNSTEIN AND SONDHEIM: *WEST SIDE STORY*

Where did Leonard Bernstein go wrong? His 1957 musical update of *Romeo and Juliet* is one of the best stage pieces yet composed by an American, and a work of enormous grasp, confidence, and insight. Had Lenny continued along these lines, who knows what he might have produced? Instead, he opted for his conducting career and his "serious" music: the dreadful *Kaddish Symphony*, the miserable *Mass*, and the awful opera *A Quiet Place*, which was intended as a sequel to the marvelous *Trouble in Tahiti*, written thirty years earlier, but which succeeded only in spoiling its memory.

I cannot say enough good things about *West Side Story*, though. From first note to last, it is brilliant. Why Bernstein slowly frittered it away—and in this regard, one is reminded of Stravinsky's crack about Richard Strauss, "The talent that was once a genius"—is a mystery best left to God and his biographers. But what an American tragedy it is.

BENNY ANDERSSON, BJÖRN ULVAEUS, AND TIM RICE: *CHESS*

Chess? Yes! The London hit/Broadway dud achieved its Platonic form in its first incarnation, the original studio recording. Despite its flaws, this is a marvelously eclectic pop score by the two men from the seventies' Swedish megagroup, ABBA. Rice, meanwhile, contributes some of his sharpest and most mordant lyrics—"Far too many jokers/Cross the border/Not a single document/In order/ Russia must be empty/Though we're all for/Basic human rights it makes you wonder/What they build the Berlin Wall for/Who do these foreign chappies think they are?" sing the weary bureaucrats in "Embassy Lament"—and "Nobody's Side" may be the ultimate expression of Rice's cheerio cynicism. Even if *Chess* never finds its perfect form on the stage, we can savor it for ballads like the "Mountain Duet," "Heaven Help My Heart," and the duet, "I Know Him So Well." Check it out, mate.

Ballets, Tone Poems, and Other Good Things

STRAVINSKY: *THE RITE OF SPRING*

Opera is not the only theatrical form that attracts composers. There is also ballet. I'm not sure why. Most ballet music is truly dreadful; sometimes I think ballet was invented to give the Adolphe Adams of the world a job. Still, some talented composers have written ballets, especially in the twentieth century, and Igor Stravinsky wrote three of them. I've put the *Rite* at the top of this list, but it's a tough call. If pressed, I might express a preference for the earlier *Petrouchka;* others might favor *The Firebird.* All three, very different though they are, are wonderful pieces and all three belong in your basic library.

The Rite, of course, is the piece that set the musical world on its ear in 1913. The riot that attended its Paris premiere is the stuff of legend and even today it is still possible to hear what all the fuss was about. This portrait of pagan Russia is one of the most rhythmically complex scores ever penned, bristling with changing meter and time signatures and cross accents; no wonder Walt Disney used it for the Dance of the Dinosaurs sequence in *Fantasia* (*now* do you remember *The Rite?*). If music were revolutionary Russia, then *The Rite* would be Lenin.

Pre-revolutionary Russia is the subject of *Petrouchka,* written in 1911 for Serge Diaghilev's Ballets Russes, just as *The Rite* was. The setting is a Shrovetide Fair, the hero is the clown, Petrouchka, and the story line concerns his hopeless love for the Ballerina. Not much, you say. But Stravinsky's extraordinarily vivid music recreates all the spectacle and pageantry of Czarist Russia, as well as humanizing his puppet characters; when Petrouchka is slain by the Moor, we are touched. When, at the end, his ghost returns and hovers over the circus, we are chilled. Rhythmically brisk, if not as complicated as *The Rite, Petrouchka* is more melodically accessible, although its harmonic signature—the famous tritone clash between C major and F-sharp major chords—is hardly anything Mozart would recognize.

So on to *The Firebird*. This is not a dance about a souped-up Pontiac, but is another primitive Russian fairy story. Stravinsky wrote it in 1910, also for Diaghilev. Of the three great ballets, it most clearly reflects the influence of Stravinsky's teacher, Rimsky-Korsakov, but it's full of spit and vinegar. The closing pages are a remarkable example of a young composer feeling his oats; you can practically hear Stravinsky exclaiming, "I can't believe I'm doing this!" Believe—and enjoy—it.

BARTOK: *THE MIRACULOUS MANDARIN*

If by now you're beginning to think I have a fondness for thorny twentieth century pieces, you're right. And this is one of the thorniest. Bartok wrote only three works for the stage: *Bluebeard's Castle* (1911), and the ballets *The Wooden Prince* (1914–16) and *The Miraculous Mandarin*, begun in 1918 but not staged because of problems with the censor until 1926. And what problems: the plot concerns a prostitute who entices lonely men up to her room; once there, they are set upon by three thugs and murdered. Her last victim is a mysterious Chinese; like Rasputin he is strangled, stabbed, hung by the neck—but he refuses to die. It is only when the girl shows pity on him that his wounds start to bleed, and he finds relief in the big sleep. Rhythmically bold, melodically biting, emotionally devastating, the *Mandarin* is a masterpiece in every way. You'll enjoy it, even if your neighbors won't.

DEBUSSY: *LA MER*

"Last night's concert began with a lot of impressionistic daubs of color smeared higgledy-piggledy on a tonal palette, with never a thought of form or purpose except to create new combinations of sounds. . . . One thing only was certain, and that was that the composer's ocean was a frog-pond, and that some of its denizens had got into the throat of every one of the brass instruments."

Nobody's perfect, not even music critics. (As you'll see in the next chapter, *especially* not music critics.) No, that is not an excerpt from one of my youthful reviews, but a considered opinion from 1907 by one Henry Krehbiel, music critic of the New York *Tribune*. Krehbiel was a Brahms guy, a Tchaikovsky guy, a Dvorak guy. Writing just two years after the premiere of *La Mer*, poor Krehbiel could not rely on Conventional Wisdom; he had to formulate his own opinion, poor guy.

Well, history has decided otherwise and no doubt were Krehbiel around today he would be making respectful noises about *La Mer*, no matter what he really thought. Indeed, he later called Debussy's great tone poem "a poetic work in which Debussy has so wonderfully caught the rhythms and colors of the sea." Deadlines, or second thoughts, or both, will do that to you.

You'll have no problem with *La Mer* (The Sea), not to be confused with *La Mere* (The Mother) or *La Merde* (The . . . oh, never mind). It's an alluring, three-movement piece, shimmering and evocative; the superb first movement is titled "From Dawn to Noon on the Sea," which caused the iconoclastic French composer Eric Satie to wisecrack, "I like the part about ten minutes to twelve." So do I.

Debussy also tried his hand at ballet in the recondite *Jeux*, which, as its name implies, is about a game: tennis, anyone? *Jeux* has never achieved the popularity of Debussy's other music—*The Afternoon of a Faun*, the *Nocturnes*, and *Images* for the orchestra, the marvelous *String Quartet*, the volumes of piano music—for its arch, enigmatic qualities consign it to the realm of connoisseurship. Indeed, late Debussy in general does not seem to be the people's choice. But you, sophisticate, should look into the three instrumental sonatas, one for violin, one for cello (both with piano, of course), and, best of all, the *Sonata for Flute; Viola and Harp*. But go gentle.

STRAUSS: *DON QUIXOTE*

On your peregrinations around the orchestral repertoire, you sooner or later will come face to face with Richard Strauss and his orchestral tone poems. Don't worry, it's perfectly natural to fall for them in a big way. After all, they're so, well, *sexy:* the awesome opening of *Also Sprach Zarathustra;* the tremendous climaxes of *Ein Heldenleben* (A Hero's Life); the frankly erotic depiction of the Strausses' bedroom activities in the *Symphonia Domestica.* In many ways, though, *Don Quixote*—don't be shocked to hear it called "Don Quicks-oat," especially by the Brits—is the best of the lot.

A deeply sympathetic musical evocation of the Cervantes novel, *Don Quixote* differs from the other tone poems in that it is a concerto for cello and orchestra. The cello gives voice to the Don, while, in the orchestra, the viola represents his sidekick Sancho Panza. Strauss the pictorialist was never so vivid as he is here: windmills turn, sheep bray, a violent storm capsizes a skiff, and the dreamy Dulcinea turns into a hag right before our very ears. The death of the Don is one of Strauss's most heartrending pages and a good performance ought to have you in tears.

From *Don Quixote* you can certainly go on to the other famous Strauss tone poems, but let me urge you to investigate the last two: the *Domestica,* mentioned above, and *An Alpine Symphony.* When I was a lad, these two were often derided and deemed unworthy to stand in line with their flashy siblings. But let me tell you, few things in music are as exciting as an all-stops-out performance of either one of these barnburners. The last ten minutes of the *Domestica* and the ascent to the mountaintop in the *Alpine Symphony* will give you goose bumps. And isn't that what music is all about?

HOLST: *THE PLANETS*

What does Mars sound like? How about Neptune? Gustav Holst, an Englishman, let us know in this 1916 suite for large orchestra. The sonic portrait of the solar system, minus Earth (where we live) and Pluto (not discovered yet), is one of music's great leaps of imagination. So what if Holst never wrote another piece like it? Nobody else did either.

Holst's music is, however, worth some exploration. Have a go at the weird *Egdon Heath* or the opera *The Perfect Fool.* If you decide to go for *The Hymn of Jesu,* though, you're on your own.

Chamber Music and Song

SCHUBERT: *TROUT QUINTET*

Franz Schubert wrote operas, too. Nine or ten of them, in fact, depending on how you count. But you don't need to know any of them; they're the worst. (At least, their librettos are; some of the music is very good.) What you do need to know about Schubert are his songs (more than six hundred, but there won't be a quiz) and his piano and chamber music. You need to know them because they're the best.

Schubert died at age 31—31!!—but he wrote a lot of music. That's basically all he did. He would get up in the morning and write like crazy, then knock off for lunch with his buddies. In the evening, there would usually be some kind of entertainment, often organized by his friends, called a "Schubertiade," a concert of Franz Peter's latest works, played by the composer himself. Imagine the discipline and dedication; most of us have barely got our feet on the ground, professionally speaking, in our early thirties; Schubert was already dead.

I've picked the *Trout*, not only because it's Schubert's sunniest piece, which is saying something, but because it neatly combines two facets of Schubert's genius: his gift for melody and his predilection for chamber music. The tune that gives the *Trout* its name is a song called *Die Forelle*, which oddly enough means "the Trout." Schubert uses the song in the five-movement work's fourth movement, as the subject of a set of variations. So the *Trout* is something of a portmanteau piece, wrapping up a lot of subjects in one glorious small package.

Although Schubert wrote nine symphonies—didn't everybody? —the poor guy didn't have much of a chance to hear them; he had to write some of them on spec, as it were. Chamber music and lieder, however, were a different story. It takes only one singer and a pianist to perform a song, just a few folks to sit down to an evening of chamber music. The *Trout* is scored for an unusual combination of piano, violin, viola, cello, and double bass (string bass, or acoustic bass, to you).

Oh, yes. The "double" in double bass has nothing to do with the number of people it takes to lug the instrument around. Rather, it reflects the instrument's origins in the continuo, which was basically the baroque rhythm section. You'll notice, when you get that far, that three people come out on stage to play a baroque sonata: the solo instrument, a keyboard instrument and, off to one side, a cellist. The cellist is the guy playing the bass line—that's all he does—because in baroque music the bass line is the most important constructive element in the piece; it's the source of the harmony.

As ensembles grew, composers in search of a deeper, richer sound began doubling the bass line with the bass; if you think of string instruments as voices, the violin is the soprano, the viola is the alto, the cello is the tenor, and the bass is, well, the bass. Anyway, at first there was no distinction between the bass and cello parts: the basses doubled the cellos. And that's why they're called double basses.

Now back to Schubert.

The *Trout* has all of Schubert's virtues. It's tuneful, it's playful, it's radiant. It's the Ms. Congeniality of music. The piano writing is dazzling, too—really hard. (Schubert was, from all accounts, only an ordinary pianist. Once, while trying to play the great *Wanderer Fantasy*—another work based on a song—he stopped and exclaimed, "Let the devil himself play this!" or words to that effect.)

With the *Trout* as your introduction to Schubert, you'll soon be ready for more. The two Piano Trios, one in B-flat major, the other in E-flat, are both spectacular; I slightly prefer the B-flat, but you may already be familiar with the slow movement of the E-flat, for Stanley Kubrick employed it in his film, *Barry Lyndon*. Even though it's from the wrong period—Thackeray's picaresque novel of an Irish social climber is set in the eighteenth century—its wistful, elegiac mood perfectly suits the movie's emotional tenor.

Kubrick, by the way, is a master at raiding the classical repertoire. We all remember how he used the opening of Richard Strauss's *Also Sprach Zarathustra* for the apeman sequence in

2001: A Space Odyssey. But don't forget the brilliant use of Beethoven's *Ninth* in *A Clockwork Orange* or, in the same film, the Rossini *La Gazza Ladra* Overture (when Alex and his droogies are beating the tar out of a rival band of thugs) and *Singin' in the Rain*, during the horrifying rape of the writer's wife. Kubrick knows that music has the power not to cloud men's minds but to move their souls, and Schubert knew it too.

If you find Schubert's piano-oriented chamber music congenial, then a whole new world has suddenly been opened to you. The Beethoven *Sonatas for Piano and Violin* (significantly, not for "violin and piano") are quite wonderful. Other favorites of mine are the piano trios of Dvorak, especially the marvelous *Dumky Trio*, as well as the *Piano Quintet*. And there is the apotheosis of piano quintets (not five pianos, of course, but a piano with a string quartet), the one by Brahms. For sheer firepower, this one cannot be topped. If you're still wondering what some people hear in chamber music, go to a performance of the Brahms *Quintet* and watch the pianist. You'll get your money's worth.

We simply must say something about the lieder. This is not the place to go into the songs in depth, but let me point you in the direction of the famous cycles, *Die Schöne Müllerin* (The Beautiful Maid of the Mill) and *Winterreise* (A Winter's Journey), two of music's crowning glories. Please read, if you can still find it, Gerald Moore's engaging autobiography, *Am I Too Loud?* The greatest accompanist who ever lived discusses these works and how to play them with the same insight and artistry he displayed in his pianism. And don't miss Schubert's *Der Hirt auf dem Felsen* (The Shepherd on the Rock), an extended song for soprano, clarinet, and piano that is one of life's little glories.

So much Schubert, so little time. But if he could write it all in thirty-one years, what excuse do you have not to listen to it?

DEBUSSY: *STRING QUARTET IN G MINOR*
RAVEL: *STRING QUARTET IN F MAJOR*

You could do a lot worse than to make these two gems your introduction to the string quartet form. Forget what you've heard about the quartet being the most "intellectual" form of music (they're talking about the Germans, not the French). Not that there is anything frivolous about either the Debussy or Ravel quartet— the first and last essays in the genre for each composer. It's just that these pieces are so fresh, so beguiling, and so intimate that all other qualities are subordinated, at first hearing, at least, to their sheer attractiveness.

This is salon music par excellence, and it positively screams fin-de-siècle Paris. The Debussy quartet, a relatively early work (it is the only Debussy composition to bear an opus number, in this case, Op. 10), came first, while the Ravel was composed about ten years later by a man twelve years his junior. The uncharitable might suggest that Ravel frankly copied the style and form of the Debussy quartet; the more broad-minded may prefer to use the French word *homage*.

Consider the similarities. A first movement in the sonata form. A second-movement scherzo marked *Assez vif—très rythmé* (Debussy); *Assez vif et bien rythmé* (Ravel). A slow movement preceded by about forty bars in which the performers all play with mutes on their instruments, producing a sultry, muffled sound. A brisk finale. Your honor, I move for conviction.

Not so fast. There are striking differences as well. The Debussy contains the famous pizzicato scherzo, inspired by the sounds of the Javanese gamelan orchestra Debussy heard at the Paris Exhibition of 1889: almost every note is plucked, not bowed. (Debussy was not the first, of course, to do this; Tchaikovsky used the same technique in the scherzo of his *Fourth Symphony*.) Ravel employs altogether brighter colors throughout his quartet; the effect is harder-edged, gemlike. (Interestingly, neither quartet is particularly "Impressionistic.") Lovers of the quartet literature are glad to have them both. We can't have the *Grosse Fuge* all the time.

Indeed, as one commentator has remarked: "Beethoven's quartets—at least, the late ones—were dramas, but Ravel's is a bustling comedy, a divertissement." Bravo.

BRAHMS: *PIANO TRIO IN B MAJOR,* OP. 8

Now here's a little number you're sure to enjoy. This trio for piano, violin, and cello bears an early opus number, but the version of it we usually hear is actually a revision undertaken some thirty-five years later. With the possible exception of the *Piano Quintet,* this is Brahms's best essay in chamber music.

You will prize the Op. 8 trio for its inexhaustible flow of melody, the brilliance and daring of its piano writing and the sheer kinetic excitement it generates. Incredibly, Brahms was criticized during his lifetime for lacking the true melodic gifts, but surely even tone-deaf critics can hear the tunes in the B major trio. The noble way the big, broad opening theme of the first movement is passed from piano to cello to violin, the way it grows and flowers and finally sings out in unison, is one of Brahms's happiest inspirations. The lightning-bolt scherzo blazes by, interrupted by a soulful, songful middle section; the adagio is deeply contemplative—Brahms in one of his brown studies—and the finale moves from a disquieted, herky-jerky beginning to a full-throated close: not in the home key of B major, though, but in B *minor.* It's Brahms at his best, and we're happily along for the ride.

BRAHMS: *VIOLIN SONATA IN G MAJOR,* OP. 78

No, wait! Did I say the Op. 8 Trio was the best of Brahms's chamber works? What about the violin sonatas? Indeed, what about them?

That's the trouble with classical music. Just when you think you've finally pinned down a favorite, along comes another piece to knock it out of the box. Of the three violin sonatas—in G major, A major and D minor—the first is sheer radiance, the second sheer amiability, and the third sheer drama. The D minor may be the flashiest, but if pressed, I'd express my preference for Op. 78. Not a trace of the great grouch here; the G major sonata is like a fireside story by a beloved uncle on Christmas Eve. Let's see: Brahms *was* a stout little man with a long flowing beard, wasn't he? Could it be?

BEETHOVEN: *THE SIXTEEN STRING QUARTETS*
THE THIRTY-TWO PIANO SONATAS

You're just going to have to bite the bullet on these, I'm afraid. Like his symphonies, there's no avoiding the Beethoven string quartets or piano sonatas. I thought I'd sneak in a discussion of the *Trout* before we got to these, so you wouldn't run away.

You'll be surprised: they're a very easy listen. Most of them, anyway. In fact, the string quartets are mostly downright enjoyable. The first six, all lumped together under the heading Op. 18, are from the early period, when Beethoven was still under the influence of his teacher, Haydn. I'm very fond of Op. 18, No. 2, the one in G major, but feel free to sample any of them; they're all fairly short.

The quartets of the middle period—generally speaking, Beethoven's most popular period—are strangely disappointing. The three *Rasoumovsky* quartets of Op. 59 are more respected than loved, although it has become a party stunt among string quartets to see how fast the finale of the *C-major quartet*, Op. 59, No. 3, can be played. They were dedicated to a Russian count—Ludwig "Rights o' Man" van Beethoven was always sucking up to royalty in his dedications—and in two of them he quotes Russian folksongs. The melody used in scherzo of the *E-minor quartet*, Op. 59, No. 2, also pops up quite prominently in the first act of Mussorgsky's opera *Boris Godunov*. So it's a small world after all. Of the other two middle quartets, my preference is distinctly for the Op. 95, called the *Serioso*. It's a fine, taut, exciting little piece.

The late quartets, by contrast, are uniformly magnificent. Everyone has his or her own favorite; mine is the A minor, Op. 132, which contains the famous *Heiliger Dankgesang* (Song of Thanks to the Deity) slow movement, one of Beethoven's most daring and moving creations. But there is also the pliant and often overlooked *E-flat quartet*, Op. 127; the incredible seven-movement *C-sharp minor quartet*, Op. 131; the graceful *B-flat*, Op. 130 whose substitute finale—the Op. 133 *Grosse Fuge* was originally supposed to be the last movement of this quartet—is the last piece Beethoven ever wrote; and the Op. 135 *Quartet in F major*, whose finale is titled "Der schwer gefasste Entschluss," which means roughly, "The grasped-with-difficulty resolution," or, better yet, "The tough question."

That sounds like trouble: Beethoven, the heaven-stormer, going out with a struggle. And, indeed, things appear pretty grim when Beethoven writes under the principal theme: "Muss es sein?" (Must it be?) "Es muss sein!" (It must be!) But the joke's on us: the *F major quartet* is a throwback almost to Op. 18, a lighthearted romp that never fails to disconcert those theorists who view a man's music as his response to the circumstances of his life. How silly a theory this is can be seen simply by considering Mozart's joyous *The Magic Flute*, written when the composer was half dead. Or the Op. 135 quartet.

About the *Grosse Fuge*. This sprawling, ugly behemoth was supposed to be the concluding movement of the six-movement *B-flat Quartet*, Op. 130. Beethoven, a laborious worker and thinker, had second thoughts, however, and as so often happened with Beethoven, his second thoughts were correct. The *Grosse Fuge* was spun off into its own opus number—in effect becoming the seventeenth string quartet—and Beethoven substituted the graceful finale that is usually used today. A grateful world thanks him.

There are twice as many piano sonatas, with a resultant unevenness about them. Beethoven was quite the pianist in his younger days, and he wrote many of his sonatas for himself to play. Like the quartets, they evolve as they go, from crisp classicism to frank romanticism—and beyond—of the last few. Indeed, the late sonatas were considered so difficult to play that it took the arrival of Franz Liszt for them to be heard in public.

A general rule: if it has a nickname, it's nice. Thus, the early *Pathetique* and *Moonlight* sonatas; you may also want to check out the *Pastoral Sonata*, Op. 28, in D major, although I find it more rewarding to play than to listen to. The middle period brings us to the splendid *Waldstein Sonata*, Op. 53—to me, the best work of the lot. Beethoven never again matched the ethereal, relaxed quality of the first statement of the finale's main theme. The thundering *Appassionata Sonata* is justly popular and the *Les*

Adieux Sonata has its partisans. The daring, two-movement *Sonata in E minor*, Op. 90, is right on the cusp, consisting of a tight, brisk opening and a long and beautiful rondo.

But the meat of the order are the last five sonatas, beginning with Op. 101. Like the late quartets, these can be deeply spiritual experiences for both performer and listeners, and they amply repay study. If you can read a score, follow along with a recording. If you can't, try to pay close attention. The finale of the *Sonata in E major*, Op. 109, is the ultimate expression of Beethoven's command of the theme and variations form; the concentrated structure of the last sonata, Op. 111 (in his favorite key of C minor) is a textbook of form.

The final exam, of course, is the so-called *Hammerklavier Sonata*. The title refers simply to the instrument upon which the sonata is to be played—the modern piano. But there is something about that word, *Hammer*, that adds an extra element to the piece. The huge four-movement work is the *Ninth Symphony* of piano sonatas, the summation of all that Beethoven had learned and discovered on his own about form and content. The piece ends with a gigantic fugue (don't be intimidated by this most "learned" of musical forms. It's just a way of organizing material logically) that taxes the resources of both performer and instrument. You won't want to hear the *Hammerklavier* every day, but break it out once a year, or on special occasions. You'll be glad you did.

BARTOK: *SIX STRING QUARTETS*

A quick word about the Bartok Quartets. Sure, they're a little rocky, like the first two piano concertos. Toughen up! Do what a real aficionado does: head straight for No. 4 or No. 5, the two avatars of Bartok's whole aesthetic. *Then* go back to the romantic ones like No. 2, which has "Made in Hungary" written all over it.

While we're on the subject of Hungarians, don't forget the music of Bartok's buddy, Zoltan Kodaly, probably best known to you as the composer of the *Hary Janos Suite*. That suite is drawn from the opera about the picaresque adventures of one Hary Janos (Hungarians, like the Chinese, present their names backwards, family names first; we would call him Janos Hary). But there is much more to Kodaly than this bonbon. If you really want to have some fun, have a listen to the *Sonata for Solo Cello;* that's right, *solo* cello. No piano, no violin, no string quartet. Just the cellist and the world's hardest piece, *mano a mano* and may the best mano win.

BACH: *THE ART OF FUGUE*

Back when we were talking about Beethoven, I asked you not to run away at the mention of the dreaded fugue. Now I'm begging you. I realize that a Bach fugue, in the abstract, may be just about the most boring—and at the same time, frightening—of musical forms. The bewigged Bach is such a stern, imposing figure that it seems that fugues, like castor oil, must be good for us if he wrote them. But there is more to Bach than fugues.

In Germany, where the public saunas are coed, I met a beautiful blond lady one afternoon and the talk turned, as the talk will when two naked people of the opposite sex get together, to music. When I asked her who her favorite composer was, she answered without hesitation, Bach. Now maybe she was just trying to impress me, but I believed her. You can love Bach; really, you can. His second wife, Anna Magdalena, certainly did: they had thirteen children together, and the rascal had seven more by his first wife! (Why did I think of that?)

The Art of Fugue is Bach's valedictory, the summation of everything he knew about music. There's a lot we don't know about it, such as why it was written and what instruments it was intended to be played on. Bach never even finished it. Still, it stands as the apotheosis of such other formidable and more familiar works as *A Musical Offering,* the piece he first improvised and later wrote down on a theme given to him by Frederick the Great at Potsdam, and the famous *Brandenburg Concertos* (which is probably where you ought to start your pilgrimage through Bach's music). Then come the great choral works, the *B Minor Mass* and, greater still, the *St. Matthew Passion.* A love of these is the mark of the sophisticate, not the tyro; don't worry if you're not ready for prime time yet. You will be, soon enough.

WOLF: *THE ITALIAN SONG BOOK*

Hugo Wolf was one of music's great crazies, but he sure could write a song. I've listed the *Italienisches Liederbuch,* but we could just as easily cite *The Spanish Song Book* or the *Mörike Lieder* (songs on text by the poet Eduard Mörike). Along with Schubert, Schumann, and Brahms, Wolf stands at the pinnacle of the German lied. Like Schubert and Schumann (but not Brahms), Wolf tried his hand at opera (*Der Corregidor*), and failed. But each of Wolf's songs are mini-operas, filled with sharply observed detail and penetrating psychological insight.

Listen, for example, to the tormented anguish of "Herr, was trägt der Boden" from the *Spanisches Liederbuch.* The serenity of "Schlafendes Jesuskind" from the *Mörike Lieder.* The friskiness of "Epiphanias," to a poem by Goethe. The tenderness of "Verschwiegene Liebe," on a text by Eichendorff. Follow a recording with the text and a good translation—you can't go wrong with the ubiquitous Dietrich Fischer-Dieskau—and delve deeply. There is a world to discover.

Some Odds and Ends

MEDIEVAL AND RENAISSANCE MUSIC

You'd be surprised how much of this you are going to like. Most of us think that music was more or less invented by the Bach family, which boasts that seventy of its members have earned their living through music since old Veit Bach staggered into Thuringia, in central Germany, from Moravia or Slovakia to the east some time in the sixteenth century. There was, however, music before Bach (Johann Sebastian), just as there was after him.

Don't expect it to sound "normal," though. The tonal system that we know and love really came together in the music of J. S. Bach. Before that, musicians wrote in modes, not keys; modes date back to Greco-Roman history (which is why they have Greco-Roman names like Aeolian, Dorian, and Phrygian), but the modes we are talking about are creatures of medieval Europe.

While I would not wish an evening of Gregorian chant on anyone, a little of it goes a long way; it is amply documented on records and you should be able to sample it fairly easily. The thing to remember about Gregorian chant is that the music was meant to serve the text, and not vice versa; no "for He shall reign for e-ver and e-e-e-e-e-e-e-ver," à la Handel, but a flexible form of sung speech. It is an ideal that Western composers like Schoenberg were still searching for a millennium later with *sprechstimme*.

A brief digression about that last term. *Sprechstimme*—literally, "speech-voice"—has occasioned a lot of confusion among musicians as to what Schoenberg really had in mind. It shouldn't be that confusing: he wanted something closer to speech than song, with the pitches just brushed lightly, not belted out. Classically trained musicians, for some reason, have had a very difficult time grasping this notion, but pop musicians can do it in their sleep. Just think of Bob Dylan. For the ideal performance of *sprechstimme*, listen to Dire Straits lead singer Mark Knopfler singing "The Sultans of Swing." Now that's *sprechstimme*.

Gregorian chant has left us with another legacy: solfege. The monks gave each note of the mode a syllable based on a hymn to St. John the Baptist: *Ut* queant laxis *Re*sonare fibris *Mi*ra gestorum *Fa*muli tuorum, *Sol*ve polluti *La*bii reatum *san*cte *Io*annes. Or, more familiarly: ut-re-mi, etc., which quickly became do-re-mi outside of France, the only country where "ut" is easy to sing.

Music developed slowly and steadily. Paris was its center at first, and the early counterpoint of Leonin and Perotin at the Cathedral of Notre Dame proved influential. The action moved to the Lowlands and Italy in the next few centuries, and the list of great composers is long. It includes Josquin des Pres, Palestrina, Orlando di Lasso, Guillaume Dufay, Obrecht, Ockeghem, and Isaac, composer of the ineffable song, "Innsbruch, ich muss dich lassen," a smash hit in its day.

Medieval and Renaissance music is a specialized taste, but you cannot go wrong by looking into the remarkable "Requiem" of Pierre de la Rue (or Pete of the Street, as his friends might have called him), Dufay's "Missa L'Homme Armé," which is based on a popular secular song of the fifteenth century, or Ockeghem's "Missa Mi-Mi," whose title does not anticipate Puccini, as the New York *Times* might suppose, but refers to the notes of the mode (see above).

Speaking of anticipating, there is one Renaissance composer you will sooner or later run into, much celebrated for his alleged "modernisms." His name is Carlo Gesualdo, Prince of Venosa, and he is famous—nay, notorious—for two things. The first is that he had his wife and her lover brutally murdered in 1590; but, then, everybody was doing that in those days. The second is his highly expressive, if not to say actually weird, madrigals and motets (vocal works for small ensemble). Stravinsky was a great admirer of Gesualdo for his use of dissonance and chromaticism, and made several arrangements of Gesualdo madrigals. Gesualdo was an extreme, though not unrepresentative, exponent of the highly ornamental Italian school of composers in the early sixteenth century. You'll enjoy his music.

And Now for Something Completely Different: Guilty Pleasures

Sometimes, no matter how you try to control yourself, you pig out on something that you just know isn't good for you. A bout with a bag of cookies, an assault on a carton of ice cream. The same goes with music. There are works you know are not masterpieces, but you don't care. You like them, and that's all there is to that.

I've got a few. Everybody does. And pretty soon you will too. So let's get the confessional ball rolling. Father, forgive me, for I listen to:

MASSENET: *WERTHER*
Yes, I know Jules Massenet is not a bona fide Great Composer. I know he's sloppy and sentimental and wrote a million operas and

right-thinking people the world over hate all of them. I know, doctor, I know. But I can't help myself: I love *Werther*.

For some reason, the French seem fond of German subjects in their operas (think of Gounod), even if it is a love that goes unreciprocated; the *Germans* are fond of German subjects, but not of French. *Werther* (say Vare-*tare*) is based on Goethe's smash novel that caused an outbreak of suicide by lovestricken young swains. Werther loves Charlotte, but she marries Albert and Werther is miserable, so he suffers a lot, sends a cryptically worded suicide note to Charlotte, and then shoots himself—on Christmas, yet. Of course she rushes to his side just too late to stop him. What a prince!

Say what you will about Massenet, but he got this one just right. The theme associated with Werther's unconsummated love for Charlotte is one of the most passionately melancholy in opera; the contrasting children's music ("Noel, Noel, Noel"), heard as Werther lies dying, is sharply ironic. (I think Berg borrowed the idea for the last act of *Wozzeck*.) Albert is suitably pompous, and Charlotte properly sexy. Even in a bad performance, *Werther* never fails to get me.

JOHANN STRAUSS, JR.: *DIE FLEDERMAUS*

I suppose we shouldn't feel guilty about liking *Die Fledermaus* (The Bat). It *is* wonderful—the first two acts, anyway. But Strauss goes so wrong in the third act—a slapstick scene set in a prison with Frosch, the drunken jailer—that it nearly ruins the magic of the first acts. Do what I do: leave after Act Two. Or just turn it off. You won't be missing anything, I guarantee you.

SHAPORIN: *THE DECEMBRISTS*

A lot of Russian music on my guilt trip, I see. This one is really from left field—from the Kirov Theater in Leningrad, in fact, which is where I encountered it for the first and so far only time in 1986. Yuri Shaporin (1887–1966) worked on his opera for thirty-three years. Like other Soviet composers of his era, he was subject to the whims of the Leader and Teacher, Stalin, and he kept revising *The*

Decembrists until it finally was performed in 1953—coincidentally, the year Stalin died.

The Decembrists is about the proto-revolution of 1825, in which a group of St. Petersburg military officers and aristocrats staged an abortive coup against the Czar. It failed, but the Bolsheviks later hailed it as a model for their own revolution a century later. Shaporin's opera is something of a kitchen-sink affair; imagine an amalgam of Borodin, Tchaikovsky, and Shostakovich. But it has a sure-handed grasp of structure, with several outstanding big scenes, and its melodies are strong, urgent, and attractive. It's still awaiting a production in the West: opera companies please take note. Record companies, too.

TCHAIKOVSKY: COMPLETE WORKS

You get the idea. Don't apologize. Enjoy. You've earned it.

SIBELIUS: *SYMPHONY NO. 2*

Amazing how reputations can suffer. Once, Finland's Jan Sibelius was considered a major symphonist; later, his music was something you wanted to put in the attic. The *Second Symphony* is a great big shaggy dog—a great big, *noisy*, shaggy dog. But it's a real bodice-ripper and conductors love it. Audiences, too.

For a not-so-guilty Sibelius pleasure, try the cryptic *Symphony No. 4*, the best of the seven. (What, no nine?)

MOERAN: *SYMPHONY IN G MINOR*

Ernest John Moeran was a minor British composer of the first half of the twentieth century. And this symphony is practically unknown in the United States; certainly, I have never heard it performed live. But even leaving aside for a moment my well-known weakness for British music, this is a glorious symphony: quirky, original, invigorating, eldritch, and eccentric in equal measure (sort of like an English Janacek). So what if the horns are too prominent, the percussion bizarre, the scherzo too short, and the finale too long? Run right out and buy it, if you can still find it (HNH Records #4014).

Moeran was Irish Protestant on his father's side, and of sturdy Norfolk English stock on his mother's. He was born in London and studied at the Royal College of Music. Wounded in the First World War, he returned to England and studied under composer John Ireland. Around 1930, he retired to the Cotswolds, where he wrote his best and most important music. He died in 1950, just short of his fifty-sixth birthday. "Good old Jack Moeran!" Neville Marriner once exclaimed to me. "Face down in the Kenmare River!" Which is, in fact, how Moeran died, apparently of a heart attack.

If you like the Moeran symphony, then by all means explore some of the other modern British symphonists: George Butterworth, composer of the lovely *A Shropshire Lad*, who was killed in World War I; Alan Rawsthorne, Arnold Bax. For a really far-out treat, look into the music of the autodidact Havergal Brian, who wrote twenty-seven symphonies *after* the age of seventy and lived to be ninety-six. What few Brian symphonies are available on disc were recorded by such less than first-rate ensembles as the Leicester Schools Symphony Orchestra. But so what? Who knows, you may even like them.

RIMSKY-KORSAKOV: *SCHEHEREZADE*

This was one of the first pieces I ever got to know, and it's still one of my favorites. Rimsky's musical evocation of the *Thousand and One Arabian Nights* is a marvelous four-movement tone poem, melodically fecund and clothed in the most glamorous orchestral raiment. There may not be a heck of a lot of content here, but who needs the *Hammerklavier Sonata* every time out?

KHACHATURIAN: *SPARTACUS*

Tacky, tacky. I know, tacky. But thrilling. Ditto the *Gayane* ballet. And the *Piano Concerto*. And the *Violin Concerto*. You get the idea. Noisy, vulgar, crass. Go for it!

ALBINONI: *ADAGIO*
BARBER: *ADAGIO FOR STRINGS*

Seen *Gallipoli? Platoon?* Then you've heard these emotive love-lies. However dubious the provenance of the Albinoni, it still sets a marvelously evocative, poignant mood, and it perfectly sums up the futility of the young Australians-turned-cannon-fodder in World War I in Peter Weir's film. The Barber, which derives from a string quartet, has become an unofficial anthem of mourning, and Oliver Stone was right in using it for his elegiac, Academy Award winning film about the Vietnam War.

MIKLÓS RÓZSA: *VIOLIN CONCERTO*

Though not many people still remember, Jascha Heifetz had a highly developed taste for kitsch, and indulged it frequently. (You haven't lived until you've heard Heifetz play Stephen Foster's "Jeanie with the Light Brown Hair.") Indeed, he was once chastised in print by a prominent critic for a repertoire that leaned too heavily on the bonbons, a tongue-lashing that he later credited with giving him the impetus to clean up his act (see, sometimes critics do some good). Even fewer people remember that Heifetz was an active commissioner of contemporary music; it is hard to imagine a violinist of equal prominence today—say, Itzhak Perlman—playing so much new music. (See the next chapter for my own tongue-lashing of performers, critics, conductors, everybody. It's not a pretty sight.)

Among Heifetz's commissions is this splendid fiddle concerto by Rózsa, first performed in 1956. Rózsa later pirated the slow movement for use in Billy Wilder's sweet 1969 film, *The Private Life of Sherlock Holmes*. In whatever form, the concerto is a wonderful piece, full of Hungarian swagger and, in the *Lento cantabile*, genuine poignancy. It's a welcome alternative to the endless round of Mendelssohns we get in the concert halls, and it is only pure snobbism that prevents modern violinists from playing it. God knows, it certainly is no worse than the Bruch *Violin Concerto* and a good deal better than anything by Henri Wieniawski. So come on, guys: give the piece a chance.

RODRIGO: *CONCIERTO DE ARANJUEZ*

I have spent the better part of my critical career avoiding classical guitar music in all its manifestations, but here I make an exception. Joaquin Rodrigo, the blind Spanish composer, never wrote a better piece than this one. You may already be familiar with the celebrated theme from the second movement: it was used in a car commercial some years ago. But don't blame Rodrigo; it could happen to anybody.

Well, that's about it for now. I realize this basic repertoire is not as basic as some might suggest. You may not have heard of even half the pieces, or half the composers, either; you may still be waiting for my views on *Bolero* and the *1812 Overture*.

If so, you're going to have a long wait. So why not toughen up now? You have those pieces if you want, any time you wish. I want you to open your mind and your ears; don't be what Charles Ives used to call a "Rollo." (Nice word, huh?) Once you have these works under your belt, you'll be ready for anything. And you'll thank me for it, too.

Now, just in case you get the idea that I unequivocally endorse everything about classical music, please proceed to the next chapter, where we take a frank and friendly look at what's *wrong* with classical music today. (Hint: a lot. Not with the music. With the people who produce it.)

INTERLUDE: BACH AND HANDEL

AT THE WALL

The Germans are really strange people. With their profound thoughts and ideas, which they seek everywhere and project into everything, they make life harder for themselves than they should.
—Goethe

At Checkpoint Charlie, the hideous maw of the Berlin Wall gapes briefly open, affording a narrow passage into the divided German soul. On its western side, a sea of sensuous color rushes down the Kurfurstendamm, past the memorialized ruins of the Kaiser Wilhelm

Church, and spends itself violently but impotently in a scatalogical orgy of graffiti against the cold concrete Anti-Fascist Protection Barrier. On the eastern side, a dour pall hangs over the city, a pall reflected in the rigorously functional, regimented gray apartment blocks that line the streets, and which even the continuing restoration of some of lost Berlin's most elegant public buildings cannot dispel. Propelled by the engine of the postwar *Wirtschaftswunder*, the capitalist Federal Republic of Germany is a sporty blonde racing along untrammeled autobahns in a glittering Mercedes-Benz or BMW. The communist German Democratic Republic, bumping along potholed roads in tiny proletarian Wartburgs and Russian-built Ladas, is her homely sister, a war bride locked in a loveless marriage with a former next-door neighbor.

Yet it is this occupied land, where reminders of Germany's defeat, shame, and partition are visible everywhere, that today is finding solace and renewed pride in its cultural heroes and native sons. On the five hundredth anniversary of his birth, the country celebrated Martin Luther. In 1985, in the year of their tercentenaries, it praised George Frideric Handel and Johann Sebastian Bach, the two greatet composers of the Baroque. Here, where the lives and paths of men like Luther, Handel, Bach, Johann Wolfgang von Goethe, and Richard Wagner intersect, the glory, unity, and tragedy of German history are a living memory.

Linked forever by a divine accident that saw them born within a month of each other in cities only eighty miles apart, Bach and Handel make an odd couple. Handel, the son of a Halle barber-surgeon who wanted his boy to study law, was a well-traveled cosmopolitan who settled in London, anglicized his name, (although he retained the German pronunciation of his surname: *Hendel*), and became the dominant operatic and oratorio composer of his day. When he died, a bachelor at age seventy-four, he was buried with pomp and circumstance in the Poet's Corner at Westminster Abbey, where his memorial plaque, oddly, has his date of birth wrong.

By contrast, Bach came from a long line of musicians, spent almost his entire life within the borders of what now is East Germany in the often contentious service of pompous princelings and severe Lutheran rectors, married twice, fathered twenty children, and died far more renowned for his organ playing than for his mostly unpublished cantatas, masses, sonatas, and concertos. Although their lives continued to intertwine at crucial points—both underwent gruesome unsuccessful, cataract surgery by the same oculist, and both went blind partly as a result—they never met.

Each age must view the past by its own light, and in our time history has drastically reversed the judgment of earlier generations. A poll taken in the mid-eighteenth century undoubtedly would have found Handel the more admired, especially in England, where his thick German-accented ghost smothered native British music for more than a century. By contrast, Bach was spoken of, somewhat scornfully, by his son Johann Christian, as "the old wig," an outdated figure working in a dying contrapuntal medium of four-part harmony and abstruse fugues.

Today, the situation has been almost entirely reversed. Handel's many operas, once so wildly popular with the London public, are infrequently performed, thanks to changing tastes and the disappearance of the castrati, the surgically altered male sopranos whose vocal power, awesome breath control, and dazzling technique stunned audiences from the Sistine Chapel to Covent Garden. Of Handel's numerous oratorios, only the redoubtable *Messiah* can be said to be really popular and his best loved instrumental works are limited to such *pieces d'occasion* as the *Water Music* or *Musik for the Royal Fireworks*. Once a dominant influence, Handel today is in danger of being popularly judged a three-piece composer. Only recently have the burgeoning original-instrument groups (most of them British) and enterprising singers begun the difficult job of restoring to the operas some of their lost luster.

Bach's music, however, has steadily grown in stature—it has even gone into space aboard *Voyager I* and *II* as an example of the best that human culture has to offer. Yet our image of Bach is, in its own way, as stodgily myopic as that of previous eras. "In Bach there is too much crude Christianity, crude Germanism, crude scholasticism. He stands at the threshold of modern European music, but he is always looking back toward the Middle Ages" said Nietzsche in 1878, as wrong about Bach as he was about Richard Wagner. But we, too, choose to perceive the cantor of St. Thomas's Church in Leipzig as, above all, an unsmiling, devout Lutheran, who erected cathedrals in sound dedicated to the greater glory of God. Bach's music, we think, is great because it is good for us. But to think of Bach as a kind of musical chaplain is to ignore the circumstances of his life, and takes no account of the roughly one hundred cantatas, many of them on secular subjects, as well as a considerable quantity of instrumental music, that have been lost. Like the Venus de Milo, Bach's legacy is a torso that has been taken to stand for the entire work, and we are largely content to keep it that way.

Perhaps we feel that way because we have so little to go on other than the music that has survived. For someone widely acknowledged as the fountainhead of German music, there is surprisingly little remaining physical evidence of Bach's existence in East Germany. The country has a plethora of preserved Martin Luther sites—Eisleben still contains both the house Luther was born in and the one he died in, and the country is dotted with the equivalent of "Luther slept here" signs—and Handel's birthplace, a solid, prosperous-looking two-story corner house, still standing on a street that was called in his day "by the Mud," is not far from his rather smug statue in Halle's central marketplace.

But almost nothing survives of J. S. Bach. His birthplace (on a street called, appropriately, the Lutherstrasse) in the hilly, wooded Thuringian mining town of Eisenach burned down long ago. In Weimar, the cultivated city of Goethe, Schiller, and Liszt where Bach's composer sons Wilhelm Friedemann and Carl Phillip Emmanuel were born, and where Bach himself spent almost a month in jail for the crime of wanting to change jobs, there is only a plaque to mark the spot where the family home stood. In Coethen, where Bach worked for the music-loving Prince Leopold from 1717 to 1723, producing among other masterworks the *Brandenburg Concertos* and the *Goldberg Variations*, the prince's castle has been largely dismantled over the years, and no one knows exactly where Bach lived. And in Leipzig, the Saxon capital of art and commerce where Bach spent the last 27 years of his life, the school in which Bach lived and taught was torn down in 1902.

Today in Eisenach, a beneficent bewigged stone figure beams down from a pedestal, quill in hand and manuscript paper at the ready; beyond it, high on a hill in the distance, sits the Wartburg castle, where Luther, in disguise, translated the Bible while hiding out from Catholic wrath. In Leipzig, a sterner Bach is memorialized outside the Thomaskirche both by a full-length statue and by a bust erected by Felix Mendelssohn on a small square not far from the church. Genius pays homage to even greater genius, for it was the romantic Mendelssohn, a Christianized Jew, who revived in 1829, a century or so after it was first performed, Bach's greatest religious work, the towering *St. Matthew Passion*. And thus unwittingly canonized him.

And this man, the greatest musical poet and the greatest musical orator that ever existed, and probably ever will exist, was a German. Let his country be proud of him; let it be proud, but at the same time, be worthy of him!
—*Johann Nikolaus Forkel* in J. S. Bach's Life, Art, and Works.
                    For Patriotic Admirers of True Musical Art.

Outside of Weimar, near a large, watchful Soviet military base, the former Nazi concentration camp of Buchenwald still stands on the slopes of the Ettersberg as a memorial to the more than fifty thousand Allied prisoners of war, German political dissidents (including Ernst Thaelmann, leader of the German Communist party in the 1930s), Slavs, Gypsies, Jews, and other undesirables who died there. Two shrunken heads are on display in a glass case, along with a tiny lampshade made out of skin and pieces of tanned, tattooed human hide that Frau Ilse Koch, wife of the death camp's commandant, found so irresistibly collectible. Vintage loudspeakers, crudely wired to the SS barracks, are silent today, but they once crackled with music as doomed prisoners ran past Koch's residence on their way to destruction.

How is it possible that the country of Bach, Handel, and Goethe could also be the country of Himmler, Eichmann, and Koch? It is a question that has vexed the rest of the world for decades, a question that the Nuremberg could not answer. Perhaps a better question might be: what other country could it have been? The Germans have long been able to hold two contradictory ideas in mind and remain untroubled by their mutual exclusivity. Only in Germany could Weimar and Buchenwald so peacefully coexist, each denying the other's nature. After all, it was the Christian monk Luther who said: "I wish and ask that our rulers who have Jewish subjects exercise a sharp mercy towards these wretched people. . . . They must act like a good physician who, when gangrene has set in, proceeds without mercy to cut, saw, and burn flesh, veins, bone, and marrow. Burn down their synagogues. . . ." It was Wagner, the composer who wrote the great Christian allegory of *Parsifal* and who chose a Jew to conduct it, who was also the author of the noxiously anti-Semitic *Jewishness in Music.*

It was also Wagner, in the same pamphlet, who said of Bach: "Just as the Sphinx strives to free its human head from an animal body, so Bach's noble countenance seeks to come forth from under its wig." This from a native Leipziger who had studied counterpoint with one of Bach's successors at St. Thomas's and who set his opera *Tannhäuser* in the Wartburg overlooking Bach's home town. "Alas! With keen endeavor I have studied philosophy, jurisprudence, and medicine, and unfortunately, theology too," says Faust in the opening speech of Goethe's play. "And yet here I stand, a poor fool no wiser than I was before!"

Sei stolz auf ihn, Vaterland! The Bach biographer Johann Nikolaus Forkel's patriotic exhortation is inscribed by a marker on the wall of Prince Leopold's castle in Coethen. If Hannah Arendt's remark about the banality of evil is true, the same might be said for the banality of genius. No one standing in the Coethen courtyard today would think that Bach could possibly have been inspired by his surroundings. The Saxon plain is as flat as Kansas, its tiny villages grim studies in brown and gray; the ferocious reforming spirits of Lutheranism and Communism have done their work well. Similarly, it is hard to reconcile Luther's tiny deathbed in Eisleben with our outsized sense of the man's historical stature. And only in Germany would there be a chart in the room where Luther died of a heart attack that enumerates his physical complaints and describes a cure he took for kidney stones that included the crucial ingredient of horse manure.

In Germany, myth and reality cross and recross: the historical Faust was Luther's contemporary, and Goethe set one of his scenes in the ancient Auerbach's Keller in Leipzig, where Luther's close friend Melanchthon claimed that in 1525 Faust rode out of the tavern on a barrel, accompanied by the devil in the shape of a dog. Today, that same Auerbach's Keller is guarded by statues of Faust and Mephisto, who is seen casting a spell over a group of Leipzig students: "Loose the bonds of illusions from your eyes!" Mephisto says as he releases them, "And remember how the Devil joked."

Bach, as vital a man as there ever was (surely his twenty children testify to that), has inevitably become part of that myth: in the Thomaskirche, his stained-glass window is right next to Luther's. In East Germany, as in most of the world, he has overshadowed his countryman Handel, who had the effrontery to defect to the West before it was politically necessary. But, thankfully, he has proved impervious to political manipulation, as Luther and Wagner have not, and resistant to the seductive devil in the German soul that caused so many others to forswear some basic tenet of humanity long before the Wall made visible what before was spiritual.

"Oh, that at long last you had the courage for once to yield yourselves to your impressions, to let yourselves be elevated, yes, to let yourselves be taught and inspired and encouraged for something great; only do not think that everything is vain if it is not some abstract thought or idea!" Goethe said near the end of his life. The triumph of Bach was that he did exactly that. The tragedy is that, even now, so few believe it, and insist on seeing the wig instead of hearing the man.

6

CLASSICAL CRISIS

WHY YOU ALWAYS THOUGHT

CLASSICAL MUSIC IS FOR

NERDS

So far, we've been discussing what's right with classical music. Now let's talk about what's wrong with it. Hang on to your hats.

It's time to admit that classical music—or, rather, the *business* of classical music—is in some serious trouble, especially in the United States. No longer solely an art, it has with each passing season become more and more of a commodity, to be packaged, sold, and marketed as if Beethoven were soap—or, better yet, a political candidate. ("I'm not a conductor—I just play one on *Live from Lincoln Center*." That sort of thing.)

Programming, once the exclusive province of the music director, has become a cooperative activity, accomplished in collusion with marketing directors and, sometimes, public relations representatives. Economics has always been a part of musical life in the United States, but today horse-trading is a way of life: of course you can play Schoenberg's cast-of-thousands choral piece, *Gurrelieder*, says the marketing director to the music director, as long as you also program Beethoven's *Fifth Symphony*. On second thought, make that maybe. On third thought, forget about it.

Not that the music director is blameless. The airplane has made the resident conductor a thing of the past. Today's prominent maestros routinely have two or even three major posts, at around half a million dollars per position, and they gad about from North America to Europe and back again in a never-ending search for a favorable exchange rate. These latter-day Flying Dutchmen—and Germans and Italians and English—are really flying carpetbaggers, contributing to the one-major-orchestra-pretty-much-sounds-like-another syndrome that makes the current orchestral scene so drab, dreary, and faceless. Gone are the days when there was a striking aural distinction between the Philadelphia Orchestra under Leopold Stokowski and the New York Philharmonic under Arturo Toscanini, or between Serge Koussevitzky's Boston Symphony and Fritz Reiner's Chicago Symphony. Today, too often, orchestras simply sound like one great big broken Deutsche Grammophon record.

Consider, for example, the 1989 flap over Daniel Barenboim and the Paris Opera. While it's true that nearly everyone eventually comes to grief at the Paris Opera (and at the Vienna State Opera, too), *L'affaire Barenboim* set a new record for greed. Barenboim, you may recall, was summarily fired as music director of the Opera Bastille, ostensibly over his round-up-the-usual-suspects programming plans for the new opera house, but in reality, two things rankled the French: 1. the outlandish size of his salary (nearly a million dollars a year) and 2. the fact that he had also signed to succeed Sir Georg Solti as the conductor of the Chicago Symphony. That job, needless to say, is not *pro bono publico.*

Now if Barenboim were the Herbert von Karajan of thirty years ago, he might have pulled it off; Riccardo Muti, after all, leads the Philadelphia Orchestra and the La Scala Opera in Milan. But by even the most charitable reckoning, Barenboim is nowhere near the first rank of modern conductors. A splendid pianist, he has been learning his podium trade at the top, as it were. And getting top dollar for it, too. As that great music lover, Gordon Gekko, said in *Wall Street:* Greed is good.

Increasingly, soloists have become caught up in keeping up. Fees, as we've already noted, can be very steep. Luciano Pavarotti has sung in some stadium concerts for which he and the company that produced the event got one hundred percent of the gross. That's right, all of it. The sponsoring organization got the prestige of having presented Pavarotti, as well as an opportunity to sell season tickets using the concert as bait. Is it any wonder orchestras and opera companies always seem to have their hands out, like high-class beggars?

The problem is, institutional classical music today is an art so divorced from its time and place that for many (not for you and me, of course) it has become a cult. Just as Catholics believe that the consecrated host is the living body of Christ, so those in the music cult believe that the standard repertoire from Mozart to Mahler is an eternal body of living art—immutable, unchangeable, a never-ending source of verity.

Notice that they never speak of a revival of *Rigoletto*, or of a Mozart retrospective, the way one does in the theater or the cinema. In their ahistorical arbitrariness, the classical-cultists are like the futuristic post-civilization society of John Boorman's film *Zardoz*, whose bible turned out to be an incomplete copy of *The Wizard of Oz* (hence the title: zardOz). Or, in their obsessiveness, like Gabriel Betteredge, one of the narrators of Wilkie Collins's detective masterpiece, *The Moonstone*, who lived his life according to precepts found in Daniel Defoe's *Robinson Crusoe:*

You are not to take it, if you please, as the saying of an ignorant man, when I express my opinion that such a book as Robinson Crusoe *never was written, and never will be written again. . . . When my spirits are bad*—Robinson Crusoe. *When I want advice*—Robinson Crusoe. *In past times, when my wife plagued me; in present times, when I have had a drop too much*—Robinson Crusoe.

Substitute Beethoven's *Fifth* for *Robinson Crusoe* and you have a pretty fair summation of the problem.

What have they done, and why? They have made a limited group of compositions into a classical canon that, arrogantly, they intend should stand for all ages. They have subjected this body of music to unremitting performance, naively assuming that it can withstand such finetoothed, Jesuitical scrutiny, when the vast majority of its creators would never have dared to make such extravagant claims for its eternal worth. Innocent of any foreknowledge of recordings, most composers expected their works to be heard only once or twice: that's why they wrote so many of them. (Compare the output of, say, Schubert, who wrote hundreds of pieces in his short life, with that of a modern composer. Big difference.) Beethoven had no idea that some day his symphonies would inspire thousands of graduate degrees in analysis, or be used to bring millions of season ticket subscribers to heel with the promise of Guaranteed Culture at No Pain. A miracle has happened: some of the most complex, innovative, and adventurous music of the nineteenth century has become nearly content-free by dint of incessant repetition. Presto: Beethoven Lite—*da-da-da-dum.*

How did this remarkable state of affairs come about? Better yet, how did we allow it to happen? The other performing arts—dance, theater, film—while far from perfect, do not exhibit the advanced atherosclerosis of classical music. There are various reasons for this. Dance, having a repertory that extends back less than a century, and having never developed a fully satisfactory means of notation, is still heavily dependent on new works and new creators. (As the use of videotape in preserving dance patterns becomes ever more expert and widespread, enabling the works of great and late choreographers like Balanchine to be accurately reproduced even without the master present, this could change.) Film too is a relative newcomer, and while it has built up a substantial body of classic work, until the advent of the home videocassette recorder, movies were not readily accessible to the general public; there was, in other words, no home film repertoire the way there is a home music repertoire. Even with VCRs, however, film audiences more eagerly rent the latest movies than old films; the market still craves novelty.

Theater, with a history and repertory even more ancient than classical music's, ought to have suffered a similar fate. But even here, revivals (clearly labeled as such) are the exception, and new plays and musicals the norm. Granted, Broadway will occasionally cast up a freak hit such as *On Your Toes* or *Me and My Gal,* but it is noteworthy that smash revivals are almost invariably musical comedies. In theater, the classic plays, from the Greeks through Shakespeare and the Restoration, coexist without animosity with the works of Samuel Beckett and Sam Shepard. There, the Old Masters do not seek to strangle their children.

Music, on the other hand, is viewed even within the profession as a practically closed circle. Although the fringes of the repertory have been gingerly pushed back beyond Bach and extended on the other end to early Stravinsky, its core has remained relatively stable; with only minor changes, the very first program performed by the New York Philharmonic in the mid-nineteenth century could be played at Avery Fisher Hall next week and no one would think the choice of music odd, old-fashioned or in any way unusual. (Do you know what one of the pieces was that the Philharmonic played back in 1842? How did you guess? Beethoven's *Fifth*.) No wonder Virgil Thomson, in his first review as a music critic for the New York *Herald Tribune*, could quote approvingly a friend's remark that the Philharmonic was not part of the intellectual life of New York. It still isn't.

Let's point some fingers and hand out some blame:

The Artist as Hero. Performers ought to serve music, instead of vice versa. Yet today the repertoire has become a kind of international track meet, with conductors and soloists competing for medals in a relative handful of events. It is possible these days to make a whole career specializing in just a few works—Klaus Tennstedt and Carlos Kleiber do—instead of displaying one's musicianship across the spectrum of musical culture. Below the professional level, things look no better: major conservatories seek to emulate past glories instead of preparing young musicians for the modern world.

The Stockholm Syndrome: the Audience as Willing Captive. The motto of today's subscribers to symphony programs can best be summed up in the famously misquoted line from *Casablanca:* "Play it again, Sam." (Just as Sherlock Holmes never says, "Elementary, my dear Watson," so the Bogart character, Rick, never actually says this.) Listeners seek art as religious experience; art as entertainment; art as anything but art. Maybe Beethoven should be banned for a while—fifty years would do nicely—so that future audiences would pick up their ears and really listen, for a change.

The Critic as Coward. From its early healthy pugnacity

("Music that stinks to the ear," wrote one prominent Viennese music critic of the Tchaikovsky *Violin Concerto*), criticism today has been reduced to a meek and mild appreciation of the status quo. From foe to friend: from the bite and bile recorded in Nicolas Slonimsky's devastating *Lexicon of Musical Invective* to the bland, bored tone of newspaper criticism today, critics have abandoned their historic role as independent watchdogs of taste and become housebroken lap dogs instead. Woof!

Recordings: A Window on the Past, or The Big Lie? One of the most pernicious movements in modern music criticism is the advocacy of the use of recordings as interpretative guidelines for contemporary performers. Because the widespread acceptance of a new technology guarantees its influence, this was inevitable. Yet arbitrary and often unrepresentative, records are only guides to the way an artist performs, not actual primary source documents. Their baleful influence has resulted in the decline of score-reading— learning the music from the notes—as some performers at least in part acquire their scores by ear. What is the difference between amateur Gilbert Kaplan's performance of Mahler's *Resurrection Symphony*, and Herbert von Karajan's? (Hint: there's a big difference.) Should composers write directly for recordings (as Morton Subotnik did with *Silver Apples of the Moon*), thus bypassing the performer's interpretive choices completely? (On the whole, probably not.) And is a composer's recorded interpretation the most authentic guide to performance, anyway? (In the cases of Stravinsky and Rachmaninoff, definitely not.)

Of these groups, may I single out my own profession for special abuse? Music criticism, as it is currently practiced in the United States, is a fraud. Indeed, it is not music criticism at all. It is *performance* criticism. When critics go to a piano recital, an opera, or a symphonic concert, they are not there to write about Liszt, Wagner, or Beethoven, except in the vaguest music-appreciation sort of way. Tacitly, they assume that every worthwhile observation about the content of Liszt, Wagner, et al., has already been made by their predecessors and betters. Instead, the modern critics' function has become to describe and comment upon the performance under examination, applying, like some journalistic Supreme Court, prevailing community standards. Their job, as it has evolved in the latter part of the twentieth century, is to discourage bizarre and willful interpretations, to ferret out artfully disguised technical inadequacies, to hold the artist to the impossibly holy standards of art. Music critics are the Brain Police of music, and very proud of it they are, too. Clearly, they have forgotten that it was—or should have been—the emotional power of *music* that first brought them into the fold, not the incunabula of performances. Musical journalism today, by and large, is not criticism, it is hagiography. No wonder much of the critics' mail comes from press agents.

One result of this foolishness has been the choking off of music's traditional lifeline—new works and new ways of playing them—by an infantile fascination with performers who must play Beethoven *just so* or their hand will get slapped. My daughter used to fly into a rage whenever I altered the words of a nursery rhyme even a little bit; this ferocious, protective orthodoxy would have qualified her for a post on any major U.S. daily, even though she was only two years old at the time. By the same token, critics and musical journalists have helped throttle music's economic health by representing it as a cabal to outsiders through both snobbishness and outright—let us use the word—nerdism. There is a reason you always thought classical music was clannish, forbidding, and arcane. They wanted you to think it was.

This is not meant to endorse ignorance. Of course we should honor our great works; of course we should honor our great artists; of course we ought to know as much as possible about the historical circumstances that gave them rise. Not to distinguish between masterpieces and lesser works is not only willful but foolhardy. And not to learn insight from the way great artists perform is the same. However, . . .

To insist that only the canon is worth playing is cultism. To insist on stylistic performance conformity is cultism. And to extrapolate performance practice from a handful of ancient recordings—by definition arbitrarily made and arbitrarily preserved—is a particularly virulent form of Zardozian cultism. Recordings, in fact, are at the heart of the problem, so all-pervasive that it is almost inconceivable that any performer now first encounters a well-known Beethoven sonata by means of the score. Or that any listener first hears the *Fifth Symphony* in the concert hall, one of the cherished bromides of conductors and administrators who need an excuse to serve up the same repertory season after season.

For the first time since concert life took recognizable shape in the nineteenth century, today's generation of performers is the only one which has had effectively zero input in the choice of repertoire and the latitudes of its interpretation. If I were starting out a career as a young pianist, I would find this attitude so appalling that I would seriously consider another, more honest, line of work. Yet remarkably, most young performers now shouldering their way out of the Juilliard School, the Curtis Institute, and the Indiana School of Music cheerfully accept this. Having grown up with tales of derring-do—what performer today wouldn't like to stick it in the eye of some cocky conductor the way Horowitz did to Sir Thomas Beecham at his American debut?—young artists want to ape their elders in every respect, and appear content to have inherited a pre-chewed and predigested repertory. The older generations were at least playing music with which they had some historical relationship—Toscanini, after all, was born in the middle of the nineteenth century and Brahms was still alive when Rubinstein was born. (The great Artur was ten in 1897, when Brahms died.) But, at the highest level of performance today, aside from Maurizio Pollini, there is hardly a pianist of note who makes new music a regular part of his art.

I once visited Claudio Arrau at his home in Douglaston, Queens. My respect for Arrau's playing of Liszt (Arrau is Liszt's pedagogical grandson) and Brahms is great. But there, on his piano, alongside the *B-minor Sonata* and the *Handel Variations*, was a work by Pierre Boulez (I think it was the *Second Sonata*). When I expressed my surprise, Arrau told me he was very interested in Boulez. But when I asked him why he did not play such music in recital, he told me his public would never stand for it.

(Gary Graffman's delightful memoir, *I Really Should Be Practicing*, begins like this: "The first time I played at the Hollywood Bowl, it was Tchaikovsky. The second time, two years later, it was the same Tchaikovsky. The third time, two years after that, I was once again told, 'Tchaikovsky.' ")

The point is that performers of Arrau's generation (see: Rudolf Serkin, Vladimir Horowitz, et al.) have become prisoners of their audience's expectations; prisoners of 57th Street, the Manhattan thoroughfare that is home to the major concert managers of America. For younger performers and conductors, the situation is even worse. Shorn of their historical imperative to seek out and perform contemporary music—indeed, to make their reputations performing contemporary music (see: Liszt, Chopin, et al.)—they have become musical eunuchs trapped in a Santayanesque nightmare that has them not only remembering history, but happily repeating it over and over again.

To deny the primacy of creativity is to condemn concert life to a continuation of its current unsatisfactory status, a ceremonial chanting of a limited liturgy, conducted by the same handful of priests for the same small congregation. We may congratulate ourselves for our exquisite taste in joining this particular sect, especially since it hides behind the facade of art or culture, but at what cost? And to what end?

What we have today is a standoff in which everyone is at fault, but no one wants—or doesn't feel he has the power—to be the one to make the first move to make things better. Conductors are not about to give up their multiple jobs for reasons both financial and emotional. Besides, in each conductor's mind lurks the certainty that he alone has cornered the market on musical truth and that therefore he deserves to bring his message to as wide an audience as possible. Nor are conductors likely to change their programming ways any time soon, no matter how much they protest against the influence of the media marketeers. How many of them, for example, are willing to end a concert with Brahms's *Third Symphony*, and forego the big noise and gratification of, say, Tchaikovsky's *Fourth?* Very few; you could look it up.

Major performers are hardly likely voluntarily to relinquish their fat fees, and they jealously guard their reserved seats at the pinnacle of their profession. Like aging athletes, they warily eye the rookies, helping the talented, blocking the brilliant. But unlike athletes, whose careers are over by age forty if not long before, musicians go on practically forever, into their seventies, eighties, and even nineties. There is not a lot of turnover at the top, nor is there a very big pool. How many certified great pianists can American concert halls accommodate at any one time? Five? Ten? Not many more. The same goes for violinists. And cellists? Two or three. Flutists? One or two. Horn players, trumpeters, violists, solo double bassists? One, maybe none. That's about it. A ghetto kid has a better chance of becoming the next Michael Jordan than a young pianist does of becoming the next Vladimir Horowitz. If there even is going to *be* a next Horowitz.

Don't expect leadership to come from the major musical organizations, either. Audiences demand to hear the same works performed in much the same way each time they enter the concert hall. Orchestras and opera companies are literally not in the business of challenging their patrons, either intellectually or emotionally. Instead, they offer the solace of the familiar. They are not selling art (once, they would have been ashamed to do even that), they are selling entertainment disguised as art.

And, God knows, don't expect the critics to lead the charge.

So: Beyond Hope or a Brave New World? Should classical music be abolished? (The conventional notion of it, that is, not the music itself.) Or should orchestras and opera companies frankly admit that they are now mostly museums, and drop all pretense otherwise? Should opera companies and symphony orchestras try to be all things to all people, or should there be some diversification in function, especially in metropolitan areas with more than one of each? There are two ways out of the programming cul-de-sac: performing unfamiliar works by dead composers and new works by living ones. Will either path be chosen? And what of the future? Will there be a continuing downward spiral as music sinks ever deeper into irrelevancy? Or is a healthy synthesis of the old and new on the horizon?

The answer, I believe, is yes. Yes to the healthy synthesis, yes to the programming alternatives, yes to specialization of ensembles. As Molly Bloom says, yes, yes, oh yes. Twenty years ago, who could have foreseen the remarkable rise of the minimalists, the acceptance of art rock in intellectual circles, the triumph of New York City's avant-garde SoHo scene, all of which restored much life and innovation to music. In many ways, serious music today is healthier than it has been in forty years. (See following Interlude.)

There is a hardy band of performers—Pollini, Pierre Boulez, David Burge—who are adamant in their belief that new music is as worthy as old. The popular and critical success of the minimalists has brought the exciting collusion of the classical and rock avant-gardes out into the open. A new generation of music critics interested in the whole range of musical experience, including rock, jazz, Third World, and folk music, is battling the cult and its myths, rediscovering the joy of classical music. Time—and history—is on our side. But we have to stay on the case.

Let's root for the good guys. This means you.

INTERLUDE: MODERN AMERICAN COMPOSERS

It rarely occurs to the contemporary composer that the blame for his estrangement from the serious music audience might lie with himself.

—Henry Pleasants, *The Agony of Modern Music* (1955)

Rarely? Make that almost never. After World War II, a special kind of arrogance took almost complete hold of creative artists worldwide, perhaps most virulently in music. Practically since the dawn of time, it had been the duty of the artist to please an audience, whether royal, bourgeois, or plebeian. Indeed, the very concept of *art for art's sake*—that is, devoid of any reference to an observer, existing in its own splendid isolation—was foreign.

The late-romantic notion of *l'art pour l'art*, however, had been the warning shot over the middle-class audience's bow, and as the nineteenth century waned, restless poets, painters, and musicians, increasingly alienated from a fundamentally bourgeois public and alarmed by the fatal course they saw history taking, ineluctably broke away from their popular roots and took refuge in what we call today the ivory tower. "My time will yet come!" cried Gustav Mahler, angered at the incomprehension with which his mammoth symphonies were first greeted. His *cri de coeur* would become the rallying cry for generations to come, justifying in one slogan the activities of the genius, the talent and the incompetent alike.

After World War I destroyed Europe's cherished cultural certainties, along with the flower of its youth and several of its sovereign boundaries, creative artists felt that their disaffection had been extraordinarily prescient. Just as the war could excise a social structure that had obtained since the Renaissance, Cubism could destroy conventional perspective and serialism could shatter the hegemony of a tonal system of musical organization that had been established by Bach. There arose the myth of the Misunderstood Artist (a myth given inadvertent credence by the protean musician, Nicholas Slonimsky, in his *Lexicon of Musical Invective*, an amusing collection of boneheaded critical assessments down through the ages; Slonimsky was not trying to make contemporary music critics even more timorous than they are, but to encourage them to sharper, even more reckless judgments, in the interests of cultural dialogue).

As the bards told it, almost every great creator had suffered the benighted hostility of a cloddish *lumpenbourgeoisie* as he valiantly overturned outdated conventions. While it is true that many important composers, artists, and playwrights have been "ahead" of their time, in that their work initially met with puzzlement and incomprehension *from some*, it is also true that most of them were appreciated, and handsomely remunerated, while they were alive.

Almost without exception, even the most adventurous artists (Wagner, for example), reviled though they were by their enemies, were also acknowledged, however grudgingly, as major figures. They were not simply ignored, as their would-be successors in the latter half of the twentieth century have been.

During the 1960s, the horizons of American music suddenly expanded, and audiences and composers found each other once again. A decade and more of the rigid theoretical and intellectual hegemony of post-Webernism was coming to an end: just as in sex, politics, and society, the watchwords became freedom, individuality, and adventurousness. Under the querulous battering of two generations of composers, the ramrod-straight dodecaphonic highway to the future shattered into a multiplicity of paths, some of which doubled back onto roads already traveled. The decline of Darmstadtism freed composers once again to give voice not only to individual styles but to individual modes of expressions; while initial reactions were tentative and uncertain, within fifteen years a thousand flowers had bloomed.

A younger generation of American composers, just coming of age in a revolutionary time, had little use for the rules and regulations of dodecaphony—twelve-tone music—as handed down by Arnold Schoenberg, refined by Anton Webern, and interpreted by Pierre Boulez, the *enfant terrible* of Darmstadt, the German city where major festivals of new music have been held since 1946; in the fifties and early sixties, Darmstadt was the place to be, attracting the cream of the avant-garde from all over the world.

Then, suddenly, on November 21 and 28, 1976, the concept of the avant-garde artist in the late twentieth century changed irrevocably. On those two days, composer Philip Glass and theater artist Robert Wilson staged their collaborative opera, *Einstein on the Beach*, at the Metropolitan Opera House in New York City, a nearly five-hour piece that defied every previous conventional notion of what an opera—indeed, what a stage work—should be. Instead of dialogue, there were only the spoken numbers One through Eight and the syllables of the solfège scale: do, re, mi, fa, sol, la, si. Instead of plot, there was a series of allusive, dreamlike tableaux, set in slow motion. And instead of music, there was Glass's relentless, pounding, repetitive amplified score, a boisterous amalgamation of rock rhythms and Asian melodic practices, the likes of which had never been encountered by a mainstream audience before. Tellingly, the Met was sold out twice for a difficult evening in the theater by two men few Americans previously had heard of.

Thus did New York City's proudly scruffy SoHo arts scene come uptown. Almost at a single stroke—although it was not realized immediately—the hegemony of the academic establishment composers of the Northeast was shattered. For years, these composers had been writing resolutely abstruse, highly intellectualized serial music that few listeners were prepared to pay to hear. Defensively, the composers asserted that their style was the result of inexorable forces, including the end of romanticism and the creation of the twelve-tone system by Arnold Schoenberg; the forces of reason and history, they said, were on their side. That audiences almost universally spurned their music did not matter. After all, wasn't it the lot of the pioneering artist to be unappreciated in his time? (And besides, they tended to be on the faculties of major universities, and thus protected from such plebeian marketplace forces as popular appeal.) Like Mahler, they felt their time would come. Their ivory tower attitude was summed up most dramatically, even arrogantly, in an essay Milton Babbitt wrote in 1958 for *High Fidelity* magazine: "Who Cares If You Listen?" It was the moral, and musical, equivalent of the New York *Daily News's* classic headline during New York City's fiscal crisis in the 1970s—FORD TO CITY: DROP DEAD.

What Glass and Wilson did was put the audience and creative artist back in touch with each other again. Since the end of World War II, the very term "contemporary music" had become practically synonymous with unpleasantness. Now here was a score that explosively combined an impeccably avant-garde theory called Minimalism with the animal urgency of rock-and-roll. It was an intellectual movement you could dance to! Although Glass and Wilson lost $50,000 apiece on the Met *Einstein*, their *succes d'estime* would prove to be, in the long run, far more tangible.

In works like *Satyagraha* (1981), an inspired meditation on the early life of Mohandas Gandhi in South Africa, and *Akhnaten* (1984), about the first monotheistic Pharoah, Glass has emerged as the leading contemporary opera composer, drawing large, enthusiastic audiences to each new premiere. Extraordinarily fecund, Glass has churned out score after score, capitalizing on the renown his earlier opera won for him to become America's leading contemporary composer for the musical stage.

In 1988 alone, Glass had three major premieres: *The Fall of the House of Usher*, which was first performed at the American Repertory Theater in Cambridge, Mass.; *The Making of the Representative from Planet Eight*, a science fiction opera that took Doris Lessing's novel as its inspiration; and *1,000 Airplanes on the Roof*, a hallucinogenic melodrama for actor and small ensemble written by playwright David Henry Hwang that had its premiere in a hangar at the Vienna International Airport. Although some worry that Glass has become too successful for his own good—and it is indisputable that Glass has a tendency to repeat himself, even in a style that is founded on repetition—in each new work Glass has forged ahead, evolving and refining a style that has made him the most exciting composer of the eighties.

His colleague and rival, Steve Reich, who effectively originated Minimalist compositional theory in such early tape pieces as *Come Out* (1966), has become a prominent orchestral composer, with commissions both in the U.S. and in Europe; Reich's *The Desert Music* was premiered in March 1984 in Cologne and brought to the Brooklyn Academy of Music late the same year. Although Glass has eclipsed Reich in public recognition in recent years, Reich has promised that musical theater will be his next venue.

It is noteworthy that both men are active as performers, as the leaders of ensembles that bear their names. In this, as in their immediate relationship with their audience, they are throwbacks to the composers of the nineteenth century, who were almost invariably the primary interpreters of their own music.

Although Wilson still remains best known in Europe, where he is regarded as one of the theater's most creative figures, the director is an unwilling expatriate. The summer of 1984 was to have seen the premiere of his twelve-hour magnum opus, *the CIVIL warS*, at the Olympic Arts Festival in Los Angeles; its cancellation for lack of funds (during an event that generated a widely remarked profit) was especially galling. Wilson's carefully wrought, exquisitely lighted stage pictures, his Freudian, non-linear sense of narrative structure, and his Wagnerian sense of time in such creations as the twelve-hour *The Life and Times of Joseph Stalin*, mark him as an important figure with an essentially non-verbal concept of theater. Wilson's art remains closely allied to music; he calls his works "operas," and frequently collaborates with leading modern composers (Glass, Gavin Bryars of Britain, David Byrne of the Talking Heads). Wilson has expanded his reach into mainstream opera, directing Marc-Antoine Charpentier's seventeenth-century baroque opera, *Medea*, in Lyons as part of a double bill that also included a modern *Medea* by Wilson and Bryars; he also has produced Wagner's *Parsifal*, a proto-Wilsonian work if there ever was one.

Lately San Francisco's John Adams (b. 1947) has emerged as the minimalist with the mostest. *Nixon in China*, Adams's incomparable meditation (to a splendidly poetic libretto by Alice Goodman) on the uses of power, sharply split critical opinion at its 1987 premiere in Houston. An opera about that *bête noire* of the liberal left, Tricky Dick himself? Mao Tse-tung as a heldentenor? A sympathetic, warm, and vulnerable Pat Nixon? It was all this and more. Adams learned his Glass and Reich lessons well, fusing minimalism to a more traditional, flexible musical language that also found room for licks from Richard Strauss and Glenn Miller in its vocabulary. Brilliant wasn't the word for it; like Glass's *Einstein* and *Satyagraha*, Adams's *Nixon in China* is one of those seminal works that will live in modern operatic history. But Adams has more than *Nixon* to his credit; such orchestral pieces as *Harmonium* and *Harmonielehre* have already stamped him as a major voice of his generation.

It is remarkable that the art of music should play such a critical part in the populist artistic revolution of the eighties. Traditionally, music has lagged behind the other arts in embracing the prevailing Zeitgeist; German romanticism, for example, blossomed in literature (Goethe, et al.) almost a half century before it took firm root in music. Although Minimalism originated in the visual arts with the work of Don Judd, Sol LeWitt, and Richard Serra, it has been in music that the movement has had its greatest effect, one that has altered the very notion of the avant-garde itself.

The concept of the avant-garde that dominated music after World War II took as its central tenets complexity, obscurity, and difficulty; at least, that is the way much of its output was perceived by listeners, who rejected it almost completely. A counterevolution was inevitable for two reasons.

The first was the natural tendency of generations to contradict each other; if complexity was the motto of the fathers, then simplicity would be the byword of the sons. The second, and more important, was the artistic necessity, and longing, for a vital relationship between creators and audiences.

Thus, the importance of an earlier generation of American composers—that generation which had been caught in the middle of the battle between the Darmstadters and an older, more conservative compositional establishment. Men like George Rochberg (b. July 5, 1918 in Paterson, New Jersey), George Crumb (b. 1929 in Charleston, West Virginia), and Jacob Druckman (b. 1928 in Philadelphia, Pennsylvania), whose music was not easily categorized, found themselves among the chief beneficiaries of the loosening of bonds, and they emerged as among the most significant figures of the sixties and seventies. In works like the *Third String Quartet* (1973), *Echoes of Time and the River* (Pulitzer Prize, 1968), and *Windows* (Pulitzer Prize, 1972), Rochberg, Crumb, and Druckman demonstrated alternative paths for the course of twentieth century music.

Although stylistically dissimilar in their choice and usage of musical materials, the three had much more in common than simply the period of their births. The tall, mild-mannered, gracious Rochberg seems an unlikely revolutionary, yet it was he, more than anyone else, who dealt the decisive blow to serialist orthodoxy in the United States. A student of Gian-Carlo Menotti at the Curtis Institute, Rochberg began as a modern mainstream composer, then becoming involved with serialism. But with *Contra Mortem et Tempus* (1965), written after the tragic death of his son, Rochberg hesitatingly but irrevocably reembraced not only tonality but the whole universe of emotional states commonly associated with it. From this "collage," which quoted stray bits of music by other composers, Rochberg eventually evolved a style predicated in part on pastiche; the explicit references to Haydn, Mahler, Bartok, et al., were meant to function not as parody but as a series of signposts pointing the way back to the (in his opinion) lost expressivity of the past.

By the time of the seminally neo-romantic *Third String Quartet* (1973), with a slow movement that might have been written by Beethoven, Rochberg had broken decisively with his own serialist roots.

My Third String Quartet comes at the end of almost twenty-five years of a ceaseless search for the most potent and effective way to translate my musical energies in the clearest and most direct patterns of feeling and thought. At the beginning of this search, I entered the world of atonality and serialism and came to terms with the musical esperanto that Arnold Schoenberg had conceived, seeking not only mastery of the syntax and craft of this special language but also its expressive possibilities. In those early years I felt a new liberation; it seemed I had found the means to say what I wanted or had to. I was convinced of the historical inevitability of the 12-tone language—I felt I was living, at the very edge of the musical frontier, of history itself.

Gradually, Rochberg became disenchanted with serialism, despite composing the magnificently dense *Second String Quartet* (1959–61). "By the beginning of the sixties," Rochberg has written, "I had become completely dissatisfied with [serialism's] inherently narrow terms. I found the palette of constant chromaticism increasingly constricting, nor could I accept any longer the limited range of gestures that always seemed to channel the music into some form or other of expressionism. . . . My Third Quartet is the first major work to emerge from what I have come to think of as 'the time of turning.' "

It is hard for us today to fully appreciate the courage of this declaration of independence. All at once, it made Rochberg a more "marketable" composer, and at the same time ruined his reputation in academe, where serialism was the favored modus operandi. The courtly Pennsylvanian came under withering fire from his colleagues, who viewed his apostasy with alarm. Still, he persevered with his new style, sending forth his *Violin Concerto*, performed by Isaac Stern, in 1974, the three *Concord String Quartets* (Nos. 4, 5, and 6), and the opera, *The Confidence Man*. The failure of the opera, based on Herman Melville's densest and most obscure novel, at its premiere at the Sante Fe Opera in 1982 marked the end of Rochberg's most fertile creative period.

Crumb, Rochberg's colleague at the University of Pennsylvania, has been heavily influenced both by his Appalachian childhood and his study with Ross Lee Finney. He is a composer of pronounced theatrical bent whose vocal and instrumental works exhibit a dark, brooding sensibility. Crumb employs conventional instruments in often unconventional ways; one thinks of the performer's assault on the instrument's innards in the *Makrokosmos* suites (an imaginative extension of "prepared piano" theory) as well as his spoken incarnations (the shout of "Christe!" in the *Crucifixus* movement), and the mezzo-soprano's flights of vocal fancy in *Ancient Voices of Children*. Like John Cage's, Crumb's scores are as much a work of art as his music, suggesting in their visual appearance the sound of the music to come. The *Spiral Galaxy* movement from *Makrokosmos, Vol. I*, for example, curls around on itself like a scorpion's tail.

Druckman, whose pedigree is Northeastern (it includes study with Vincent Persichetti and Peter Mennin at the Juilliard School in New York City and with Aaron Copland at Tanglewood), is even more explicitly theatrical. His work at the Columbia-Princeton Electronic Music Center, which he began in 1965, showed him the expressive possibilities of technology, especially when used in conjunction with live performers. In works like the *Animus* series, and particularly in *Animus II* for female voice, two percussionists and tape, Druckman's predilection for the dramatic gesture is clearly evident; *Animus II* is a melodrama in which a flirtatious, seductive mezzo arouses aggressively sexual feelings in the percussion battery. Of *Animus III*, for clarinet and tape, the composer has written: "[the work] presumes that the theatrical and musical elements are inseparable; that the ideal performance of the music already embodies the performance of the drama."

In the works of both men, the world of the imagination figures prominently. Druckman's prize-winning orchestral piece, *Windows*, employs carefully defined aleatory, which demands that the musicians listen to one another as they improvise. (In the same way, the *Viola Concerto* (1978) demands that the soloist contribute his own temperament to the musical mix, to use all his guile and wiles to circumvent "the terrible power of the full orchestra," as Druckman has put it.) *Windows* also demands imagination on the part of the listener. Of this piece, Druckman has said:

The "Windows" of the title are windows inward. They are points of light which appear as the thick orchestral textures part, allowing us to hear, fleetingly, moments out of time—memories, not of any music that ever existed before, but memories of memories, shadows of ghosts. The imagery is as though, having looked at an unpeopled wall of windows, one looks away and senses the afterimage of a face.

Scraps of more conventional music—half-remembered waltzes here, a chorale there—float through the score, glimpsed as the windows open briefly. Despite its somewhat forbidding exterior, *Windows* is a warmly romantic score, and one that repays the listeners many times over for the active use of his mind.

If anything, Crumb takes us even deeper into the dark realm of memory and the unconscious, often approaching the condition of the primal scream. Not by accident are all his vocal works from the period 1963–1970 based on the haunting poetry of Federico Garcia

Lorca, and indeed Crumb considers them a cycle: *Night Music I*, the four books of *Madrigals; Songs, Drones and Refrains of Death; Night of the Four Moons;* and *Ancient Voices of Children.* Crumb's penchant for harrowingly descriptive text-setting is given full rein in these works. One thinks immediately of the *Casida del Herido por el Agua* (*Casida of the Boy Wounded by the Water*) from *Songs, Drones and Refrains of Death* (1968), which the composer has said is his favorite of all the Garcia Lorca poems he has set over the years. At the words, "What a fury of love, what a wounding edge, such nocturnal murmurs, such a white death!" the music erupts in fury and the baritone howls in the pain of ecstatic, almost Wagnerian, oblivion.

Similarly, the first two books of *Makrokosmos* take full advantage of the capabilities of the solo pianist, including his (they should really be performed by a man to achieve their full effect) vocal resources. The player is called upon to sing and whistle, in addition to providing such percussive effects as rapping the piano's metal structural beams with his knuckles. And there is a dizzying array of other special effects as well, including placing a sheet of paper or a metal chain on the strings and (in the spectacular *Phantom Gondolier* movement from *Makrokosmos, Vol. I*) playing on the strings with thimble-capped fingers. Crumb also makes use of quotation, as when, in *NightSpell I* from *Makrokosmos, Vol. I*, he instructs the pianist to whistle phrases of the revival hymn, *Will There Be Any Stars in My Crown?* And, inevitably, the ancient Latin sequence of the *Dies Irae* flits through his music—in the *Prophecy of Nostradamus* movement from *Makrokosmos, Vol. II*, for example, or the amplified string quartet, *Black Angels.*

Although none is in the forefront of today's avant-garde, Rochberg, Crumb, and Druckman remain significant figures in American music. By and large, their major works all have been recorded, and Crumb's works for solo piano are firmly in the repertoires of such ambitious pianists as David Burge and Robert Miller. Rochberg's daring break with serialist orthodoxy opened the door for Glass and the Minimalists to rush through in triumph a few years later, and restored respect to the key of C major. In sonic imagination and expansion of instrumental techniques, the music of Crumb and Druckman also has proven highly influential; it codified many of the advances of the late 1950s and early 1960s and transformed them from the experimental to the lingua franca of composers all over the world. Perhaps most important, though, the music of all three men is directly, viscerally communicative. One needs to know no theories, nor subscribe to any school of thought to enjoy it. Emerging from an overly politicized era, that may be its greatest accomplishment.

Their achievement, and that of Glass, Reich, and Adams as well, was to reestablish the sense of partnership and mutually shared adventure that is the historical norm for artists and audiences. The Northeast academic composers (Donald Martino, Charles Wuorinen, et al.) who had claimed the mantle of the avant-garde during the post-Webern years, were, with the possible exception of Elliott Carter, driven for cover, there to sulk, adapt, or die.

We began with a quote from Henry Pleasants's seminal, *The Agony of Modern Music*, a slender bombshell that daringly exploded the preconceptions of the postwar musical establishment.

Thirty years later, the agony finally is ending.

7

WHERE—AND HOW—DO I START?

Now it's time for me to deliver. I know you think that what we've been doing so far was all in good fun. But here comes the part where we put it all together, and answer your deepest, most heartfelt questions. Such as: which concerts should you go to? How do you decide which records to buy? With which artists? Stuff like that. (A few hundred pages back, I made fun of you for putting George Winston on the turntable at parties: see Appendix B for some practical alternatives.)

The Socratic method is not enough for you, I see. You want me to draw you a picture. And here I thought you were Plato. Well, be warned.

Warned that my taste and yours will not always coincide. That reasonable men and women may differ. That I may even be wrong.

Yes, wrong. Let me tell you about a fan letter I got once, years ago, when I was a critic in Rochester. Every critic gets letters: a few of praise, a million of blame. I tell you, you have to be able to take it as well as dish it out in this dodge. "Dear Mr. Walsh," it began, and that was the nicest part. "You are the epitome of the world's most nauseating vermin, forever spreading filth and disease amidst your footsteps." And then it really got nasty. "Not even a thunderbolt would want to touch your leprous cerebellum," went one line. "The list of mistakes you have made publicly would make any mother weep that you were born to show your face upon this earth," or some such.

But it was the final peroration that really won my heart:

"Someday your sins will find you out and that will be a sad day for you, Mr. Walsh, but a happy day for the demons who will welcome you to the steampits of Hell with screams of fiendish delight! Woe to you!!"

(Notice how easily I quote this letter from memory. Most artists will tell you that they never read reviews, but that is a dirty lie. They not only read them, they *memorize* them; years after I savaged them, a singer or instrumentalist will come up to me and start reciting chapter and verse from a review they never even saw! It's amazing.)

Up to this point, my admiration for the writer knew no bounds. But, like many fans intent on having the last word, my anonymous correspondent—for, alas, so he or she was—tore the letter from the typewriter, then reinserted it (not quite getting it to line up properly) and leveled me with one final, vulgar blast: "You are a jackass." (You'll get your chance, too.)

So let's begin. Where shall we start?

How about with the subject I've been trying to avoid from the beginning? With records. Okay, you asked for it.

I am ambivalent about records. On one hand, they have immeasurably added to our store of knowledge about the musical repertory. Think about it. At your fingertips, you can have an aural knowledge of music from Machaut to Todd Machover. You can know the Beethoven symphonies or the Brahms string quartets in a way that no nineteenth century listener could. Without venturing from a seat in your living room, you can command the greatest opera singers in the world to perform for you. That's great.

On the other hand, recordings have immeasurably subtracted from our appreciation of live performance. Because we have accepted the no-flaws mentality of the record producers and recording engineers, we now expect note-perfect readings of the standards from our performers, and make technique the very first thing we listen for, however unconsciously, in performance. A pianist like Artur Schnabel, who sometimes dropped bunches of notes—not to mention most of the nineteenth century virtuosos— would be in big trouble today.

So recordings: a net positive or negative? A mistake, or did He do it to us on purpose? I frankly don't know. I wouldn't trade my record library for a lifetime pass to all the orchestras and opera companies in the world. (Well, maybe I would. On second thought, naaaaaahhh. . . .) But I can see the dangers they pose for the future, not the least of which is the crippling effect they have had on young performers today.

But on the theory that if you can't beat 'em, join 'em, here are some random thoughts on record purchases:

1. *Go to your record store and buy some records.* Not too many at once. If you've been casting an eye on your local symphony orchestra programs for the season, buy a recording of one of the pieces you might possibly hear at a concert. Study it. Then go to the concert. Unlike movies or most novels, a musical work becomes more enjoyable the more it is heard, up to a point. While it is true that you can enjoy the *Eroica* on first hearing, it becomes far clearer on second, tenth, and eighteenth hearing. It takes time for the ear to become used to the sounds, and here recordings give us tremendous leverage. Given the wealth of recorded material, there is no need to encounter any standard work cold—unless, of course, you want to.

2. *If you're not cramming for a concert, buy something that appeals to you.* In Chapter Five, I introduced you to a lot of music. Pick a few works from that list and try them. There's no money-back guarantee attached, I'm afraid; tastes are just too different. You may despise some of the modern music I've selected, or you may consider pre-Schoenberg impossibly, troglodytically retro. How am I to know? But how are you to know, either, until you try?

One of the reasons I haven't provided record recommendations heretofore is that the industry is in just too much flux right now. The LP is going the way of the dodo bird and, as it does, a great deal of repertoire is being dropped from the catalog. Some of it may eventually resurface on compact disc, but there's no way to predict—except to note that, in general, the more obscure the material or the performance, the less likely it will wind up on CD.

And this means a lot of the most interesting LPs will go down the drain while routine Eugene Ormandy performances stagger on to their next incarnations.

Still, you are entitled to some guidance, so here goes:

A TOTALLY ARBITRARY, THOROUGHLY OPINIONATED GUIDE TO (SOME) PERFORMERS IN WHICH A FEW PROMINENT ARTISTS, BOTH LIVING AND DEAD ARE ASSESSED AND SOME REPUTATIONS SULLIED

CONDUCTORS

Arturo Toscanini: the Big Enchilada. Love him or hate him, you can't avoid him or his reputation. I'm inclined to the latter camp, but he invented the modern school of conducting. Colorful, too. *Porco miserio!*

Wilhelm Furtwängler: the yang to Toscanini's yin. Slow (sometimes) instead of fast (sometimes); spiritual instead of glib; boring instead of penetrating. (It all depends on where you sit.) Like most stereotypes, partly true. A great Wagnerian. For a real roller-coaster ride, get your hands on Furtwängler's wartime recording with the Berlin Philharmonic of Schubert's *Ninth Symphony*. You won't believe it.

Herbert von Karajan: the man some love to hate. The furor over Karajan's Nazi party membership during the Hitler years has long since died down, allowing him to be appreciated for his considerable musical gifts. Karajan is very good in nineteenth century romantic music: Beethoven, Brahms, Bruckner, Mahler, Wagner. He is very bad in Mozart; ironically, because Karajan, like Mozart, was born in Salzburg.

Georg Solti: "Sir Georg" to you. His eagerly awaited *Ring* at Bayreuth in 1983 was one of the epic disasters of modern opera production. But his London recording of the cycle in the 1950s and 1960s sure was great.

Eugene Ormandy: music's utility infielder. Good orchestra builder, although the "Philadelphia sound" died with him.

George Szell: another Hungarian named George. Renowned for his Mozart, although it sounds thin and lumpy to me on records. But folks who heard him live swear by Szell's performances. Maybe you had to be there.

Leonard Bernstein: the *enfant terrible* is past seventy now, the grand old man of American music. Once known for his great Haydn, and good (but, in hindsight, overrated) Mahler, he is now celebrated for his bathetic Brahms. Go figure.

Pierre Boulez: the only genius personally known to me. The avant-garde composer doesn't want to conduct any more, which is the world's loss. Come back to the podium, Pierre. Your art form needs you.

James Levine: the erstwhile operatic *wunderkind* has settled into his mid-40s, improving every day. Terrific in the operatic repertory practically across the board, although his taste in singers remains erratic and willful. Less accomplished in the symphonic repertory, although his Mahler symphony cycle has some splendid moments, especially the *Third*.

Carlos Kleiber: son of the sainted Erich. Born in Berlin, grew up in Argentina. Sure, demands a zillion rehearsals, is distressingly prone to cancellation, and only seems to know a handful of pieces. But what a handful!

Claudio Abbado: the fiery Italian does very well by fiery Italian music—Verdi and the like. But he knows his way around the German repertoire too. Idiosyncratic at times, but always interesting.

Riccardo Muti: another Italian, not so fiery. Chilly, in fact. They love him in Philadelphia. They would.

Bernard Haitink, Edo de Waart: two dull Dutchmen. There hasn't been an exciting Dutch conductor since Willem Mengelberg.

De Waart is quite good in Rachmaninoff's orchestral music, though.

Colin Davis, Andrew Davis: two dull Englishmen; as a general rule, all conductors named Davis are dull.

Seiji Ozawa: Do's: the Franco-Russian bonbon repertoire, from *Capriccio Espagnol* to *Bolero*. Don'ts: everything else.

Lorin Maazel: the cold fish of conductors. If only there were music by Eskimos.

Zubin Mehta: nobody buys his records; why should you? Should have stayed in Los Angeles.

Daniel Barenboim: the spiritual son of Wilhelm Furtwängler, at least in his own mind. Summarily fired as music director of the new Opera Bastille in Paris, only to be named Solti's successor in Chicago a few days later. Hard to understand what all the fuss was about. Nice pianist, though.

PIANISTS

Vladimir Horowitz: the greatest high wire act in piano history. Unbeatable in Liszt and Rachmaninoff; idiosyncratic elsewhere. But always fascinating.

Artur Rubinstein: gone but not forgotten. Probably the best all-around pianist—and *musician*—who ever lived. You can't go wrong with a Rubinstein recording.

Claudio Arrau: the patrician pianist's pianist. Some find him boring; I find him thrilling. Untouchable in Beethoven and very tough in Brahms and Liszt, although not flashy like Horowitz.

Rudolf Serkin: hell of a Brahms player in his salad days. Exciting Beethoven, too. Father of Peter.

Sviatoslav Richter: widely admired Russian pianist, but still a banger, in the mold of so many Soviets. Bangs up a storm in the Mussorgsky *Pictures*, though.

Vladimir Ashkenazy: from Mozart to Rachmaninoff, can do it all. Potentially major conductor, too.

Maurizio Pollini: intellectual Italian with a wide-ranging repertoire. A force of good, if a little cool at times.

Krystian Zimerman: the best of the younger generation, and a worthy successor to his fellow Polish countryman, Rubinstein. If only he would play more. Chopin and Brahms are his meat.

Emanuel Ax: dutiful but a little, well. . . . Call him Emanuel Zzzzzzzzzzz.

Alfred Brendel: very classy. Earnest like Arrau, catholic (small "c") like Rubinstein, and a great Mozartean. With apologies to Murray Perahia, Brendel's recordings of the Mozart piano concertos are the ones to get.

Glenn Gould: late, great and more than a little crazy. Terrific Bach; you simply must have his *Goldberg Variations.*

VIOLINISTS

Jascha Heifetz: the best who ever lived—or who ever will live. Yes, he played a lot of junk, and yes, he was a meanie in his private life. But could that man play the fiddle!

Nathan Milstein: Horowitz's buddy from the old Russian homeland. A class act.

Isaac Stern: exasperating. Sometimes he's the best and sometimes he's the worst, depending on whether he's been practicing or saving Carnegie Hall. The greatest tone of all time.

Shlomo Mintz: like Perlman, another Israeli. Looked like he was going to inherit the Heifetz mantle, at least as far as sheer technique is concerned. He still may. Or may not.

Pinchas Zukerman: yet another Israeli-born violinist. The poor man's Perlman, he has branched out as a violist and conductor. Good taste in contemporary music; plays a mean Berg concerto.

Itzhak Perlman: you don't have to be Jewish to play the violin, but it sure seems to help (see above list). Lots of talent, slightly frittered away in recent years. Wonderful tone, though.

Anne-Sophie Mutter: German. Beautiful. Fabulous player. You would gladly pay hard-earned money to hear her. Or just watch her change her strings.

Kyung-Wha Chung: from Korea. Shared the Leventritt prize in 1967 with Zukerman. Big sound, solid technique, good sense: ought to be more highly regarded than she is.

Cho-Liang Lin, Mi Dori, et al.: you don't have to be Asian to play the violin, but it sure helps.

CELLISTS

Gregor Piatigorsky: like everybody else, fled Mother Russia for the U.S.A. Played chamber music with Heifetz and Rubinstein. There really were giants in the earth in those days.

Pierre Fournier: the great French cellist, who died in 1986. His recording of the Dvorak concerto with Szell and the Berlin Philharmonic, issued on Deutsche Grammophon, remains the one to have.

Janos Starker: Hungarian. What technique; hearing Starker play the Kodaly *Sonata for Solo Cello* is one of music's most dazzling displays.

Mstislav Rostropovich: For a conductor, he was a great cellist. Now, except for Russian music, the Peter Principle in action.

Yo Yo Ma: may have the best cello technique of anyone around, past or present. Born in Paris to Chinese parents, as all-American as apple pie. Talent to burn, an engaging personality—the sky's the limit for Yo Yo. Not to be confused with "Yo, Mama!" a term found in rap music.

OPERA SINGERS

(There are hundreds of important singers, past and present, and each one, it seems, has his or her partisan. The following is just a brief consideration of some of the more famous modern voices.)

Leontyne Price: for my money, the lady you want to hear in the big Italian (read: Verdi and Puccini) repertoire when the money is on the table. The finest Aïda of our time, the best Leonora (in *Forza*), the quintessential Tosca. . . . Well, you get the idea.

Joan Sutherland: had her admirers, not including myself. La Stupenda, they called her, and she sure could hit the high notes and float a pianissimo. But there is much more to opera than that; no one could understand a word she ever sang.

Birgit Nilsson: the lady did Wagner. And how. To a whole generation, she *was* Brünnhilde and Isolde, not to mention Salome and Elektra in Richard Strauss's operas of the same name. **Kiri Te Kanawa:** Great voice. Dull singer. Gets worse the more she sings a part; try to hear her debuts in a role. **Marilyn Horne:** born to sing pants-role mezzo parts. Technique like machine gun fire. A throwback to the great days of bel canto, when men were men and men were women too; only now it's the women who take the men's roles. And "Jackie" takes them. **Luciano Pavarotti:** a.k.a. Lucianissimo, the Great One, the Fat Man, the King of the High C's, etc. Not what he used to be, but who is? Get him in his prime, in the early and mid-seventies: the *La Boheme* with Karajan will do nicely. Now you know what all the shouting was about. **Placido Domingo:** his hated rival. Never had the sheer beauty of voice that Pavarotti did, but has outlasted him through sheer hard work and solid musical sense. Nice guy, too. Might turn into a conductor someday.

This obviously is just a small sampling of the many artists who have recorded. Now it's time for a quick thumbnail assessment of who's good for what (conductors; instrumentalists, singers):

Bach: Gustav Leonhardt; Glenn Gould.

Haydn: Karajan, Bernstein, Neville Marriner.

Mozart: Christopher Hogwood, Trevor Pinnock, Bruno Walter, Sir Thomas Beecham; Brendel, Perahia; Pilar Lorengar, Benita Valente (sopranos), Frederica von Stade (mezzo).

Beethoven: Karajan; Arrau.

Schubert: the Beaux Arts Trio; Elly Ameling (soprano), Dietrich Fischer-Dieskau, Hermann Prey (baritones).

Chopin: Rubinstein, Vladimir Ashkenazy.

Liszt: Arrau, Brendel, Earl Wild, Jorge Bolet.

Brahms: Istvan Kertesz; Rubinstein, Arrau, Julius Katchen; Szeryng, Josef Suk.

Verdi: Abbado, Karajan, Levine; Leontyne Price, Margaret Price, Domingo, Sherrill Milnes.

Tchaikovsky: Bernstein.

Bruckner: Karajan, Haitink, Jascha Horenstein.
Mahler: Bernstein, Karajan, Levine, Walter.
Wagner: Solti, Karajan, Furtwängler, Boulez.
Debussy: Boulez.
Stravinsky: Boulez, Bernstein.
Shostakovich: Rostropovich, Bernstein, Maxim Shostakovich.
Schoenberg, Berg, and Webern: Boulez, Karajan; Suk (Berg Concerto).

A few final thoughts about record buying:
You don't have to spend a fortune. Every major label has reissues, which they package and sell cheaply. A whole generation of music lovers grew up listening to obscure German orchestras like the Southwest German Radio Orchestra on Turnabout. If you're on a budget, check out the cheaper labels. After all, it's the *music* you're after, not the performances. Right?

Don't be afraid to consult the record review column in your local newspaper, or read the record review magazines. When I was growing up, I leaned heavily on *High Fidelity* and *Stereo Review* for education and guidance, but the media conglomerates that own those publications have pretty much wrecked them by now, so you are on your own.

Now then, what about television and the radio?

Most every major city and town has its own classical music station. Some of them are quite good. There are also the various National Public Radio stations, which offer some classical programming. With the proliferation of cable, TV now offers things like the Arts and Entertainment Network, and there are always old standbys like *Live from Lincoln Center* and *Live from the Met*, although the unavoidable New York centrism of those shows is severely limiting.

You get the picture. But what about live concerts? You're probably still a little intimidated by all those guys up on stage in their monkey suits. Not to mention the people in the audience in *their* monkey suits. You don't even own a monkey suit. Or a monkey dress, for that matter.

What, still scared? After all the icons we've smashed? Remember, concert-going (a terrible word, but we seem to be stuck with it) is supposed to be fun. And stretching is supposed to be a gentle exercise, but it still hurts like hell.

Fun, I say. And it *is* fun. Just start small. You don't have to buy a full season's worth of tickets to your local orchestra, although they'd certainly like you to.

Why?

Because the single-ticket buyer can't be trusted to show up the next week, that's why. As a result, orchestras across the country have bought Danny Newman's "Subscribe Now" philosophy of aggressively selling subscriptions. This way they know what their deficit's going to be in advance, instead of being surprised by it at the end of the season.

There is, however, a serious flaw in this reasoning: no one knows how many people—just like you—have been discouraged from attending a concert because they couldn't get a ticket to the one program they wanted to hear. A subscription audience's taste is the most predictable thing in the world, and this in part accounts for the timorous programming orchestras have been inflicting on the musical public in recent years. How is an orchestra's management supposed to know there are dashing, adventurous, inquisitive people like you out there if you never show up and make your voice heard? If you never write to your local critic and tell him—sorry, feminists, it's almost always a him—to get off his duff and start doing his job? If you're not part of the solution, then you're part of the problem.

Anyway, most orchestras offer various sampler series, small blocks of four or five concerts chosen from the full season. They're a good way to get your feet wet. And if you really never have heard a warhorse like Beethoven's *Fifth*, then you are precisely the person orchestral conductors and marketing directors are forever invoking as they lamely defend their programming philosophies: "There's always someone in the audience who has never heard Beethoven's *Fifth*," they claim piously, as if that explained everything. I've never met that person, but if you are he (or she), please raise your hand. Isn't it great to be special?

The point is, relax. Give it time. Nothing worthwhile happens immediately; Rome wasn't built in a day, or a week, or even a year. But Rome's still around, which is more than can be said for the Pruitt-Igoe housing complex in St. Louis. Instant gratification and quick-fix solutions just don't work.

This goes, I know, against the current ethos of corporate America, which seeks Results Now and is likely to get Apocalypse Tomorrow instead. It takes years to learn the repertory, and even then there is always one more piece of music to hear, another new work to discover, a premiere to attend. Becoming a music lover is, in fact, the never-ending story. It is baseball instead of football, bodybuilding instead of weightlifting, unlimited by the clock and ever seeking higher levels of personal attainment. If you're a short-term, goal-oriented middle manager, get out of here; if, on the other hand, you agree with Robin Williams—"Infinity: what a concept!"—then classical music is for you.

Think of the future. You can now plan your week around going to a certain concert or opera, preparing at first at home with a recording, score, or libretto. Instead of wasting your time in France trying to get into a three-star restaurant, save the money and buy a ticket to the Paris Opera; even if, as planned, the opera company has moved to the Bastille, the Garnier Building alone is worth the price of admission and you can always endure a ballet for one evening.

If, as might well happen, you become a diehard Wagnerite—don't blame me; I've warned you—then you can drive yourself crazy trying to get tickets for the Wagner Festival some summer at Bayreuth. (Hint #1: write well in advance and then pray your number comes up. Hint #2: bring money.) While you're in central Europe, you might also want to consider cashing in your life savings for a pair of tickets to the Salzburg Festival, down the road in Austria.

Or you may just want to stay at home and spin a few discs on the old CD spieler. Don't feel the slightest bit guilty: as history proves time and again, technology once developed will invariably be used, whether for good or ill. You are simply in tune with the historical Zeitgeist.

In the end, though, you are going to be a happier person. That
is the bottom line. (Come on back, short-term, goal-oriented
middle managers. All is forgiven.) God knows, there are a lot of
people walking around this earth who have never heard *The
Marriage of Figaro* or *Carmen* or the *Ring* cycle and think
themselves none the worse for it. But a love for this and other
music expands your intellectual horizons—just think of how much
smarter you're going to feel when you are able to discuss leitmotifs
without flinching; it's almost like rocket science!—and deepens
your emotional capacities. You want a caring, sharing relationship:
here it is.

Remember when I said that classical music wouldn't necessarily
make you a better person?

I lied.

EPILOGUE

Okay, so I lied. Please forgive me; it was for your own good. We've come a long way together, and I hope it has been fun. It's just that I didn't want to scare you off before you gave classical music a chance.

And you did! Whether you keep up with it or not is up to you. But you can't say you're not ready for it now. Congratulations.

We've discussed a lot of repertoire, touched on a number of composers' lives, glanced off some of the Big Issues facing music today. But if there's one thing I'd like you to take away from this book, it's my guiding principle: to think about, care about, and love *music*, not performers.

Anybody can be a fan. And anybody is. You see them at the opera, rushing brazenly down the aisles to throw bouquets of flowers at some fading diva whose best notes are many, many years behind her. (Who *are* these people?) You see them standing ostentatiously at concerts, screaming "Bravo" (and accenting the second syllable) at some broken-down pianist reduced to depending on his audiences' memories of past glories for his present remuneration. (Who *are* these people?) You hear them arguing violently at intermissions, getting into fistfights with the standees, all over some perceived slight or other to some cult figure or other. Who *are* these people?

Not our crowd, dear. We view music as the sport of the gods—not Mars, but Jupiter. When we choose a concert or opera to attend, we do so on the basis of what is played, not the player: it is the work that excites us, that fires our imagination, that drives us mad with desire. When we go to Bayreuth, it is for the *Ring*ing, not the singing. Even if we're only going downtown to our local symphony, it's to hear the Berg *Violin Concerto* or the Franz Schmidt *Fourth Symphony*, not to hear Mr. Perlman play the Tchaikovsky concerto one . . . more . . . time. . . .

Further, we view classical music not as a self-contained, self-referential coven of initiates, but as one element in the larger sweep of European and American culture. Music is not our lives. It is a part—albeit a very important one—of our lives, but we keep it in context.

We are not content to repeat over and over, "Beethoven is a great composer," without understanding why that statement is true—and without understanding why at times it is *not* true, too. We descry the effect of Wagner on his contemporaries—and on ourselves as well. And we realize the importance of music regaining its good health and vitality in our own time, that it may survive, live long and prosper. We do not want the tombstone to read: Classical Music 1685–1945. We want a future, not just a past.

And that, my friends, is up to you.

So who's afraid of classical music? Not you anymore. You're one of us now.

APPENDIX A: DEALING WITH THE SNOBS

Think of this chapter as a handy reference chart. As we've seen, a lot of things in classical music are simply assumed and not explained or, sometimes, even discussed. Well, here they are:

Composer's Names...

Whom You Want	What He's Also Called (or Spelled)
J. S. Bach	Sebastian Bach
Bela Bartok	Bartok Bela (Hungarian)
Ludwig van Beethoven	Luigi van Beethoven (Italian)
	Louis van Beethoven (French)
George Frideric Handel	Georg Friedrich Händel (German)
Joseph Haydn	Franz Joseph Haydn
Franz Liszt	Liszt Ferenc (Hungarian)
Felix Mendelssohn	Jakob Ludwig Felix Mendelssohn-Bartholdy.
Giacomo Meyerbeer	Jakob Liebmann Beer (his real name)
Jacques Offenbach	Jakob Eberst (his real name)
Sergei Rachmaninoff	Sergey Rakhmaninov (British usage)
Robert Schumann	Florestan, Eusebius (his *noms de plume*)
Richard Wagner	Richard Geyer (as a child)
Anton Webern	Anton von Webern

. . . and Their Pecadilloes

Bach	Sex (20 children), pride, temper
Beethoven	Sex (mostly futile), personal hygiene, temper
Berg	Sex (affair with married woman)
Brahms	Sex (with prostitutes), bad temper
Chopin	Sex with transvestite (George Sand [a woman])
Debussy	Sex (French, wasn't he?)
Janacek	Sex (affair with much younger married woman)
Liszt	Sex (made Mick Jagger look like a monk)
Mozart	Money, dirty jokes, billiards
Mussorgsky	Booze
Puccini	Sex (multiple adulteries)
Rachmaninoff	Humorlessness, crewcut
Saint-Saens	Sex (homosexual pederasty)
Schubert	Sex (died of syphilis at age 32)
Schumann	Mental health (went mad, jumped in Rhine, died of syphilis)
Smetana	Sex (went deaf, went mad, died of syphilis)
Tchaikovsky	Sex (homosexual)
Verdi	Sex (lived in sin with Giuseppina)
Wagner	Sex (with friends' wives), greed, anti-Semitism, crypto-fascism, welshing on debts, hemorrhoids
Wolf	Sex (went mad, died of syphilis)

Some Well-Known Works That Sometimes Hide Under Other Names

What You Want	What It's Really Called (or Where It's From) And Its Other Names
BACH:	
The Well-Tempered Clavier	*Das Wohltempierte Klavier*
BARTOK:	
Bluebeard's Castle	*A Kekszakallu Herceg Vara*
BEETHOVEN:	
Moonlight Sonata	*Sonata No. 14 in C-sharp minor*, Op. 27 no. 2. (*Sonata Quasi una Fantasia*)
Eroica Symphony	*Symphony No. 3 in E-flat major*, Op. 55 *Heroic Symphony* (British)
Beethoven's Fifth	*Symphony No. 5 in C minor*, Op. 67
Pastoral Symphony	*Symphony No. 6 in F major*, Op. 68
Choral Symphony	*Symphony No. 9 in D minor*, Op. 125
BERLIOZ:	
Symphonie Fantastique	*Symphonie Fantastique* *Fantastic Symphony* (British)
BORODIN:	
Strangers in Paradise	(*Prince Igor*)
CHOPIN:	
I'm Always Chasing Rainbows	*Fantasie-Impromptu*, Op. 66
COPLAND:	(*Appalachian Spring*)
The Gift to be Simple	
DEBUSSY:	
Afternoon of a Faun	*Prelude a l'Apres-midi d'un Faune*

The Girl with the *Flaxen Hair*	*La Fille aux Cheveux de Lin*
DUKAS:	
The Sorcerer's *Apprentice*	*L'Apprenti Sorcier*
DVORAK:	
New World Symphony	*Symphony No. 9 in E minor* *Aus dem neuen Welt*
de FALLA:	
Ritual Fire Dance	*(El Amor Brujo)*
Nights in the Gardens *of Spain*	*Noches en los Jardines de España*
The Three-Cornered *Hat*	*El Sombrero de Tres Picos*
GLUCK:	
Dance of the Blessed *Spirits*	*(Orpheus et Eurydice)*
GOUNOD:	
Faust	*Faust* *Margarete* (German)
HAYDN:	
Surprise Symphony	*Symphony No. 94 in G major*
Drum Roll Symphony	*Symphony No. 103 in E-flat major*
JANACEK:	
Jenufa	*Její Pastorkyna* (its real name)
MENDELSSOHN:	
Fingal's Cave	*The Hebrides Overture*, Op. 26
Italian Symphony	*Symphony No. 4 in A minor*, Op. 90
MOZART:	
Jupiter Symphony	*Symphony No. 41 in C major,* K. 551
The Marriage of *Figaro*	*Le Nozze di Figaro* *Figaros Hochzeit*
The Magic Flute	*Die Zauberflöte* *La Flute Enchanté*

MUSSORGSKY:
Pictures at an Exhibition — *Bilder einer Ausstellung*
RACHMANINOFF:
Prelude — *Prelude in C-sharp minor, Op. 3 No. 2*
Full Moon and Empty Arms — *(Piano Concerto No. 2 in C minor, Op. 18)*
ROSSINI:
The Thieving Magpie — *La Gazza Ladra*
SAINT-SAENS:
Organ Symphony — *Symphony No. 3 in C minor, Op. 78*
SCHOENBERG:
Transfigured Night — *Verklärte Nacht*
SCHUBERT:
Trout Quintet — *Quintet in A major, Forellen*
Death and the Maiden — *Der Tod und Das Mädchen*
Cello Quintet — *Quintet in C major*
SCHUMANN:
Spring Symphony — *Symphony No. 1 in B-flat major*
Rhenish Symphony — *Symphony No. 3 in E-flat major*
SCRIABIN:
The Poem of Ecstasy — *Poéme d'Extase*
JOHANN STRAUSS, JR.:
Die Fledermaus — *Die Fledermaus* / The Bat (British)
The Gypsy Baron — *Der Zigeunerbaron*
A Night in Vienna — *Eine Nacht in Venedig*
Tales from the Vienna Woods — *Geschichte aus dem Wienerwald*
The Beautiful Blue Danube — *An der schönen blauen Donau*
Emperor Waltz — *Kaiser-Walzer*
RICHARD STRAUSS:
Death and Transfiguration — *Tod und Verklärung*

Till Eulenspiegel's Merry Pranks	*Till Eulenspiegels lustige Streiche*
Sinfonia Domestica	*Domestic Symphony* (British)
STRAVINSKY:	
The Rite of Spring	*Le Sacre du Printemps*
The Fairy's Kiss	*Le Baiser de la Fée*
The Firebird	*l'Oiseux de feu*
	Der Feuervogel
TCHAIKOVSKY:	
Pathetique Symphony	*Symphony No. 6 in B minor*
	Pathetic Symphony (British)
VAUGHAN WILLIAMS:	
Sea Symphony	*Symphony No. 1*
A London Symphony	*Symphony No. 2*
Pastoral Symphony	*Symphony No. 3*
Sinfonia Antarctica	*Symphony No. 7*
VERDI:	
A Masked Ball	*Un Ballo in Maschera*
The Force of Destiny	*La Forza del Destino*
Don Carlos (French)	*Don Carlo* (Italian)
VIVALDI:	
The Four Seasons	*Il Quattro Stagioni*
	Die Vier Jahreszeiten
	Les Quatres Saisons
WAGNER:	
The Ring Cycle	*Der Ring des Nibelungen*
	L'Anneau du Nibelung; La Tétralogie (French)
	The Nibelung's Ring (British)
The Flying Dutchman	*Der Fliegende Holländer*
The Valkyrie (British)	*Die Walküre*
The Twilight of the Gods	*Götterdämmerung*
	Les Crepuscle des Dieux

Transcriptions and Arrangements

Sometimes composers get it into their heads to monkey around with someone else's—or even their own—work. They like to think they're improving it. Sometimes they do. You be the judge.

Work	Original Source
BACH:	
Four Organ Concertos	Vivaldi's *L'Estro Armonico* and other sources
BACH-BUSONI:	
Toccata and Fugue in *D minor*	Bach's original for organ (arranged for piano)
MOZART:	
Messiah	Handel's *Messias*
MUSSORGSKY-RAVEL:	
Pictures at an *Exhibition*	Mussorgsky's piano version (for orchestra)
RAVEL:	
Le Tombeau de *Couperin* *Sonatine* *Pavane pour une Infante* *Défunte* *Valses Nobles et* *Sentimentales*	Ravel's original piano versions
SCHOENBERG:	
Piano Quartet (orchestral version)	*Brahms Piano Quartet in G minor,* Op. 25

APPENDIX B
PRACTICAL USES FOR CLASSICAL MUSIC

You probably have never heard of *Gebrauchsmusik*, but I'm going to inflict it on you now. Don't worry, though; it's painless.

Gebrauchsmusik simply means "useful music," a term popularized by the twentieth century German composer Paul Hindemith. Hindemith, who wrote several million sonatas for divers instruments, almost none of them performed today, intended his pieces in the old tradition of *Tafelmusik* or *Hausmusik*—that is, practical compositions that people could play in their homes. We, however, mean something quite different. Something *really* useful:

Sunday morning brunch: Baroque and early classical. This is what God invented Telemann for. Also: Vivaldi's *Four Seasons*, Handel's *Water Music*, and various *Concerti Grossi*. Bach's *Brandenburg Concertos*. The first ninety or so of the Haydn symphonies. Mozart's early works. Sunday morning brunch is the only time during the week when you will ever want to hear a trumpet concerto.

Dinner parties: Chamber music. Mozart, Haydn, and Schubert piano trios and string quartets. The Op. 18 string quartets by Beethoven. Schubert's *String Quintet*. See also: Sunday morning brunch.

Seductions: What if, you know, you've invited an attractive person of the opposite sex over and you just want to slip something comfortable on the turntable? Depends on what kinds of music you find sexy. Few, however, can resist the siren song of the following: Schoenberg's *Transfigured Night*, the *Prelude and Liebestod* from Wagner's *Tristan und Isolde*, Vaughan Williams's *Tallis Fantasy*, the third act of *La Boheme*, the Chopin *Nocturnes*, Elgar's *Sea Pictures*, the Quintet from *Die Meistersinger*, the Adagietto movement from Mahler's *Fifth Symphony*, and *Les Illuminations*, Britten's song cycle for female voice based on poetry for Rimbaud. And you know what? *Scheherezade* is not bad, either. You'll find things on your own soon enough, I promise. After all, necessity is the mother of invention.

Exercise: Wagner's overtures to *Rienzi* and *Tannhäuser*. Baroque music of the "sewing-machine" school: Telemann, Vivaldi, etc. The first movement of Mozart's *Prague Symphony*. Unlike rock, though, classical music tends to change moods rapidly, which prevents building up the ostinato head of steam you need in jazzercise classes. Still, for limited applications, classical makes a nice change of pace. So to speak.

Working: You may not be among the lucky ones who get paid to listen to music while they work, but a good tune *does* make the time pass more quickly and pleasantly. Look at it this way: a Mahler symphony will kill an hour, and the first act of *Götterdämmerung* alone will take the better part of two hours. Before you know it, it's time for lunch!

Driving: Depends on where you're going. I wouldn't try to fight Manhattan traffic with anything short of the Talking Heads or the Kinks, but for mellower motoring experiences, classical music offers a world of variety. Try to match the mood of the music to the landscape. When cruising the Alps or the Rockies, put Schubert's *Great C-major Symphony* on and thrill to the opening bars' magnificent invocation of nature. (Richard Strauss's *Alpine Symphony* also works nicely in this regard.) At sunup, Strauss's *Also Sprach Zarathustra* will resonate with cosmic harmony, as Stanley Kubrick discovered. Heading across Nebraska, the Bruckner symphonies will keep you company nicely. For cross-country trips, the *Ring* makes a nice traveling companion. (Although I must admit that rock-and-roll is still the best driving music ever: Steppenwolf's *Born to Be Wild,* for example, or Jimi Hendrix's *All Along the Watchtower.*) Still, the opera of your choice is always right: who can forget Al Pacino in *Serpico* crossing the Brooklyn Bridge while singing along with Puccini's *Gianni Schicchi* at the top of his lungs? No law says you can't do it too.

Mood Music: Whether you're in a brown study or ready to jump for joy, music seems to intensify feeling. Maybe we've just been conditioned by a century of moviegoing, but it's hard to imagine an emotional state without an accompanying soundtrack. The Soviet Union for years has used an orchestral arrangement of the Funeral March movement from the Chopin *Piano Sonata No. 2* to signify the passing of its leaders; in Germany, "Siegfried's Funeral March" from *Götterdämmerung* means the same thing, while in the United States Barber's *Adagio for Strings* has gradually come to be associated with national mourning.

A broken heart in a love affair can be assuaged, if not consoled, by Werther's pathetic arias in Massenet's eponymous opera; at last, here is someone who feels worse than you do. For women, the cognate is Tatiana's Letter Scene in Tchaikovsky's *Eugene Onegin*. Expressions of great joy, on the other hand, range from the heavy artillery fusillade of Beethoven's "Ode to Joy" (the finale of the *Ninth Symphony*) to the simple, whirling abandon of Johann Strauss, Jr.'s "Roses from the South" and "Emperor" waltzes. Remember, no matter what your mood, some composer has been there before you.

APPENDIX C
HOW TO BRANCH OUT FROM THE PIECES YOU ALREADY KNOW

Think of this chart, a companion to Chapter Five, as your guide into the great unknown. Do you enjoy the work in Column A? Then head for the pieces in Column B. It's that simple. Before you know it, you'll be making up your own charts.

The Basic Repertoire

Composer and Work	Alternatives
BACH: *The Art of Fugue*	BACH: *Brandenburg Concertos* *The Musical Offering*
BARTOK: *Bluebeard's Castle*	BARTOK: *The Wooden Prince* (ballet) *The Miraculous Mandarin* (ballet)
BEETHOVEN: *Eroica* Symphony *Violin Concerto*	MAHLER: *Symphony No. 3* BEETHOVEN: *Pastoral Symphony* *Piano Concerto No. 4*

String Quartets (16)	BARTOK: *String Quartets* (6) SHOSTAKOVICH: String Quartets (9)
Piano Sonatas (32)	BRAHMS: Piano Sonatas (3)
BERLIOZ: *Symphonie Fantastique*	ORFF: *Carmina Burana* SAINT-SAENS: *Danse Macabre* LISZT: *Totentanz* RIMSKY-KORSAKOFF: *Scheherezade*
BERG: *Violin Concerto* *Wozzeck*	BERG: *Lyric Suite* (string quartet) *Lulu*
BIZET: *Carmen*	BIZET: *The Pearl Fishers* DELIBES: *Lakme* MEYERBEER: *l'Africaine* *Robert le Diable*
BRAHMS: *Symphony No. 2*	BRAHMS: Symphonies Nos. 1, 3, and 4 DVORAK: *Symphony No. 7* RAFF: *Lenore Symphony*
Piano Concerto No. 2	BRAHMS: *Violin Concerto* DVORAK: *Cello Concerto*
Piano Trio, Op. 8	BRAHMS: *Piano Quintet* Violin Sonatas (3)

BRITTEN:
Death in Venice
	BRITTEN: *Billy Budd*
	    Peter Grimes
	    Les Illuminations (song cycle)

BRUCKNER:	BRUCKNER: Symphonies 4, 6, 7, and 8
Symphony No. 9	
DEBUSSY:	DEBUSSY: *Images for Orchestra*
La Mer	DEBUSSY: *Sonata for Flute, Viola, and Harp*
String Quartet	RAVEL: *String Quartet*
SIR EDWARD ELGAR:	
Symphonies Nos.	ELGAR: *Cello Concerto*
1 and 2	*Violin Concerto*
HOLST:	
The Planets	JANACEK: *Sinfonietta*
	BARTOK: *Concerto for Orchestra*
MAHLER:	
Symphony No. 9	MAHLER: *Das Lied von der Erde*
	Resurrection Symphony
	TCHAIKOVSKY: *Pathetique Symphony*
MENDELSSOHN:	
Italian Symphony	MENDELSSOHN: *Symphony No. 3*
OLIVIER MESSIAEN:	
Turangalila	PHILIP GLASS: *Satyagraha* (opera)
Symphony	MENOTTI: *The Medium* (opera)
	JARRE: *Lawrence of Arabia* (film score)
MOZART:	
Symphonies	HAYDN: Symphonies
Piano Concerto,	MOZART: *Piano Concerto, K.* 466
K. 595	*Piano Concerto, K.* 488
The Marriage of	*Così fan tutte*
Figaro	*Don Giovanni*
	The Magic Flute
MUSSORGSKY:	
Boris Godunov	MUSSORGSKY: *Khovanshchina*
	BORODIN: *Prince Igor*
ORFF:	
Der Mond	ORFF: *Oedipus der Tyrann*
	BRITTEN: *Curlew River*

PUCCINI:
La Boheme   PUCCINI: *Tosca*
                                    Madama Butterfly
                                    Turandot
                           MASSENET: *Werther*
                           CHARPENTIER: *Louise*
SCHUMANN:
Symphony No. 2   SCHUMANN: Symphonies 1, 3, and 4
IVES:
Symphony No. 2   IVES: *Symphony No. 3*
                           MACDOWELL: *Piano Concerto No. 2*
                           MOERAN: *Symphony in G Minor*
JANACEK:
Jenufa   JANACEK: *Katya Kabanova*
                                    The Makropoulos Case
                                    From the House of the
                                       Dead
PROKOFIEV:
Violin Concerto   TCHAIKOVSKY: *Violin Concerto*
No. 1
SCHUBERT:
Trout Quintet   SCHUBERT: Piano Trios Nos. 1 and 2
                                    String Quintet
                                    Die Schöne Müllerin
                                    Winterreise
SHOSTAKOVICH:
Symphony No. 15 SHOSTAKOVICH: *Symphony No. 5*
Lady Macbeth of   *The Nose*
Mtzensk
                           SHAPORIN: *The Decembrists*
SIBELIUS:
Symphony No. 2   SIBELIUS: *Symphony No. 4*
JOHANN STRAUSS, JR.:
Die Fledermaus   STRAUSS: *The Gypsy Baron*
                           LEHAR: *The Merry Widow*

RICHARD STRAUSS:
Don Quixote STRAUSS: *Ein Heldenleben*
Also Sprach Zarathustra
An Alpine Symphony
Symphonia Domestica
STRAVINSKY:
The Rite of Spring STRAVINSKY: *Petrouchka*
The Firebird
PROKOFIEV: *Scythian Suite*
KHACHATURIAN: *Spartacus*
Gayane
TCHAIKOVSKY:
Piano Concerto RACHMANINOFF: *Piano Concerto*
No. 1 *No. 3*
Piano Concerto No. 2
LISZT: Piano Concertos Nos. 1 and 2
VAUGHAN
WILLIAMS:
Symphony No. 5 VAUGHAN WILLIAMS: Symphonies Nos. 2,
3, 8, and 9
The Pilgrim's Progress (opera)
Serenade to Music (choral work)
The Lark Ascending (violin and orchestra)
VERDI: VERDI: *Rigoletto*
Don Carlos
Otello
Falstaff
PFITZNER: *Palestrina*
WAGNER:
Die Meistersinger WAGNER: *Tristan und Isolde*
Der Ring des Nibelungen
LORTZING: *Zar und Zimmermann*
WOLF:
The Italian WOLF: *The Spanish Songbook*
Songbook *Mörike Lieder*

INDEX